**Slide Rule
for
the Mariner**

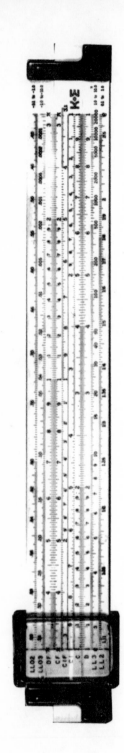

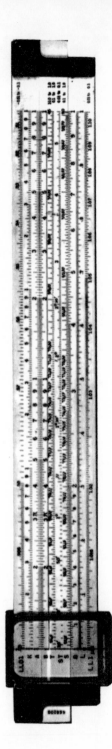

A 10-inch K & E Log Log Duplex Trig Slide Rule

Some slide rules graduate angles in degrees and minutes of arc, while others graduate them in degrees and decimals of degrees. Since a considerable portion of this book is devoted to problems in navigation, in which angle is customarily expressed in degrees and minutes, a rule of the former type, as shown here, was used in preparing the various problems.

However, a slide rule graduated in decimals can be used equally well for all problems, including those in the field of navigation, if the user bears in mind the fact that 0.1 degrees equals 6.0 minutes. Conversion of decimals of degrees to minutes, and vice versa, is discussed in the section on *Graduation of Angles*, pages 7 and 8.

Slide Rule
for
the Mariner

H. H. Shufeldt
Captain, USNR (Retired)

Naval Institute Press

Annapolis, Maryland

APR 1 7 '73

Copyright© 1972
by the United States Naval Institute
Annapolis, Maryland

Log Log Duplex Trig is the registered trademark of the
Keuffel & Esser Company

Library of Congress Catalog   Card Number: 74-188008
ISBN: 0-87021-655-4

Printed in the United States of America

To my constant companion
afloat and ashore
the Log Log Duplex Trig Rule

1745190

Preface

During World War II and for a couple of years thereafter, I served as navigator in an aircraft carrier and as commander of various types of ships. Thus, I was almost constantly involved in navigation. At times, particularly after the war, the Navy was very shorthanded and the work load was heavy. It was during these years that I discovered how much time could, on occasion, be saved by use of the slide rule. Many mathematical operations at sea can be performed with acceptable accuracy and more expeditiously with the slide rule than with any other means usually available. Furthermore, the slide rule permits a rapid check for gross errors in long, conventionally worked calculations.

This book contains examples of problems that are most readily solved with the slide rule, and of others that are most readily solved by other means but for which the slide rule can be used when the best means is not available. In addition, it includes two methods of fixing position by observations of a single body. These are given only as a matter of possible interest to the navigator, as instrumentation of sufficient accuracy to permit their successful use afloat is not yet available. The book does not by any means cover all the work that can advantageously be done afloat with the slide rule, and the reader may enjoy discovering a lot more.

For emergency use, long-term Sun and Star almanacs are provided. Given accurate time and a sextant, they will permit reasonably accurate celestial navigation, particularly if observations are made at low altitudes.

It is assumed that the reader is familiar with the slide rule, including the sine, tangent, and sine-tangent scales. However, a brief review of the

vii

use of the rule is included, as is a short section on plane and spherical trigonometry.

Most readers undoubtedly use a 10-inch rule, as I do. In the preparation of the examples for this text, however, it seemed expedient to use a 20-inch Log Log Duplex Trig rule, manufactured by the Keuffel & Esser Company. A magnifying lens over the hairline on the sliding indicator proved to be very helpful.

H. H. S.

CONTENTS

OFFSHORE NAVIGATION

MISCELLANEOUS COMPUTATIONS

Slide Rule
for
the Mariner

Review of Procedures

Use of the Slide Rule

Since this review of the use of the slide rule must be brief, it is strongly recommended that any reader who is not reasonably proficient in the use of the rule read the handbook supplied with each rule by the manufacturer, and run through the exercises it gives.

This book is intended for use with a 10- or 20-inch slide rule, having the following scales: **A**, **B**, **C**, **CI** (**C** Inverted), **D**, **K**, **S** (sine), **T** (tangent), and **ST** (sines and tangents of angles of about 0° 34′ to 5° 44′). It was prepared on the assumption that the reader would be using a rule on which the **S**, **T**, and **ST** scales are graduated in degrees and minutes of arc, as the values of angles in navigation are customarily so stated. However, should he use a rule of the "decitrig" type, on which the **S**, **T**, and **ST** scales are graduated in degrees and their decimals, all he need do is convert the decimals, where required, to minutes, a simple operation explained under **S and ST Scales.**

The basic scale on the slide rule is the **D** scale: it is divided into nine primary parts, numbered 1 (left index), 2, 3, 4, 5, 6, 7, 8, 9, and 1 (right index), and graduated so that each number represents the log of that number. The **C** scale is identical to the **D** scale.

Inspection of the **C** and **D** scales shows that the space between any two primary marks is divided into ten parts by nine secondary marks. Further divisions are furnished by tertiary marks: on the 10-inch rule, each tertiary mark between 1 and 2 represents .01; between 2 and 4, it represents .02; and between 4 and 1, it represents .05. In reading the scales, interpolation by eye is required between any successive pair of tertiary marks. With the 10-inch rule, we read to four figures on part of the scale, and to three on the remainder. Allowing for an error in reading of one-tenth of the smallest interval on the **D** scale, an answer read from this scale should be accurate to no less than about one part in a thousand. This is sufficient to give acceptable results in solving many problems; where greater accuracy is required, the slide rule gives a good check on an answer obtained by more precise solution.

Multiplication

To find the answer to the multiplication of two numbers, it is necessary only to add their logs in the following manner:

To multiply 2 by 4, set the left index on the **C** scale against 2 on the **D** scale, and move the glass indicator so that the hairline is on 4 on the **C** scale. Under the hairline, read the answer, 8, on the **D** scale.

To multiply 5 by 4, set the right index of **C** to 5 on **D** and, with the hairline moved to 4 on **C**, read 2 on **D**. Mental arithmetic indicates then that the answer is 20.

The problem to be solved dictates which index of the **C** scale should be used. For example, had the right index been used in the first example above, 4 on **C** would have been off the **D** scale, and the result would have been the same had the left index been used in the second example. In cases such as these, all that is necessary is to move the hairline to whichever index of **C** is on the **D** scale, slide the **C** scale so that its other index is under the hairline, and read the answer on **D** under the appropriate value on **C**.

The sines and/or tangents of angles may be multiplied in a similar manner.

When multiplying decimals, disregard the decimal points and place them by approximation after obtaining the preliminary answer from the rule. For example, to multiply 27.7 by 2.13, under the hairline on **C**, read 59. Mental arithmetic indicates that, since 27 multiplied by 2 equals 54, the answer must be 59.0.

Similarly, to multiply 0.00206 by 17.5, under the hairline on **D**, read 3605. Since 0.002 multiplied by 17 equals 0.034, it can be deduced that the answer is 0.03605.

Division

The **C** and **D** scales are used for division also, but, for that purpose, instead of the log of one number being added to that of the other, as in multiplication, one log is subtracted from the other. To divide 6 by 3, set 3 on the **C** scale to 6 on **D**, and under the left index of **C**, read 2 on **D**. Again, either index of **C** may be used. If 30 is to be divided by 4, the answer, 7.5, is found on **D** under the right index of **C**. In division, as in multiplication, the decimal point is placed by approximation.

Combined Multiplication and Division

Where the product of two numbers is to be divided by a third number, the operation can be performed in one setting of the rule. For example, to solve $\dfrac{6 \times 3}{4}$, all that is required is to set 4 on **C** over 6 on **D**, and then under 3 on **C**, read 45 on **D**, which is written as 4.5.

CF and DF Scales

Many slide rules carry **CF** (**C** Folded) and **DF** (**D** Folded) scales. These are identical to the **C** and **D** scales, except that their indices are placed at about the center of each scale, and the symbol π (approximately 3.1416) appears at the ends of the scales. Note that when the index of **CF** is set to any number on **DF**, the index of **C** is set to the same number on **D**.

Proportions or Ratios

Proportions, or ratios, are equivalent to equations. Thus

$$\frac{2}{5} \times 4 = 1.6$$

can be written as

$$5:2::4:1.6$$

It is frequently more convenient to solve an equation as a proportion. For example, X in the formula

$$\frac{0.762\,X}{4.95} = 4.62$$

could be found by stating

$$X = \frac{4.62 \times 4.95}{0.762}$$

However, it would be simpler to solve for X by treating it as a proportion and writing

$$4.95:0.762::X:4.62$$

Then, with 4.95 on **C** over 0.762 on **D**, over 4.62 on **D**, read 3 as the value of X on **C**. A moment's consideration enables the value of X to be established as 30.0.

CI and CIF Scales

CI and **CIF** are inverted scales, with markings like those of the **C** and **CF** scales, but in reversed order. Therefore, they can also be described as reciprocal scales.

The regular processes of multiplication and division are reversed when these scales are used. Thus, if 2 on the **CI** scale is set against 3 on **D**, under the index of **CI** (and/or of **C**), read 6 on **D**. Similarly, if the index of **CI** is set against 8 on **D**, under 2 on **CI**, read 4 on **D**.

This permits the multiplication of three numbers with only one setting of the slide. For example, to multiply $3 \times 2.5 \times 6$, set 2.5 on **CI** against 3 on **D**, and under 6 on **C** read 45 on **D**.

A and B Scales

A and **B** scales, which are identical, are useful for working with squares or square roots of numbers. They are double scales, in that they are divided into two equal portions, and "1" appears at the center, as well as at each end.

To find the square of a number, it is necessary only to set the hairline to that number on the **D** scale and read the square under the hairline on **A**.

To find the square root of a number between 1 and 10, the hairline is set to that number on the left half of the **A** scale, and the answer is read under the hairline on **D**. To find the square root of a number between 10 and 100, the same procedure is followed, except that the hairline is set to that number on the right half of the **A** scale: for a number between 100 and 1,000, the left half of **A** is used, the right half for numbers between 1,000 and 10,000, and so forth.

The square roots of decimals between 0.1 and 0.999 are located on **D** below the given decimal on the right-hand portion of **A**, while the square root of a decimal between 0.01 and 0.0999 is found on **D**, below the decimal on the left-hand portion of the **A** scale. For example, to find the square root of 0.02, set the hairline to 2 on the left-hand portion of the **A** scale, and read 1415 on **D**, which would be written 0.1415.

The **B** scale, being located on the slide, can be used in conjunction with the **D** scale for multiplying and dividing a number by the square root of another number.

K Scale

The cube of any number on the **D** scale will be found directly above it, on the **K** scale, which is divided into three equal portions. Conversely, the cube root of a number located on the **K** scale will be found directly below it, on **D**. The left-hand portion of the **K** scale represents numbers between 1 and 10, the center portion those from 10 to 100, and the right-hand portion, those from 100 to 1,000. This cycle is repetitive, as with the **A** scale.

To find $\sqrt[3]{3}$, set the hairline to 3 on the left-hand portion of **K**, and read 1.44 on **D**; $\sqrt[3]{30}$ appears on **D** under the 3 on the center portion of **K**, and is read as 3.11; while $\sqrt[3]{300}$ appears as 6.7 on **D**, under 3 on the right-hand portion of **K**.

To obtain the cube root of a decimal, move the decimal point to the right three places at a time until a number between 1 and 1,000 is obtained, and set the hairline to this number on **K**. Note the corresponding number under the hairline on **D**, then move the decimal point to the left one-third as many places as it was moved in the original operation.

Thus, to find $\sqrt[3]{0.00054}$, proceed as though finding $\sqrt[3]{540}$, and find 8.14 on **D**. Then, moving the decimal point two places $\left(\dfrac{6}{3}\right)$ to the left, find that $\sqrt[3]{0.00054}$ is 0.0814.

S and ST Scales

The graduations on the **S** and **ST** scales represent angles. These scales are, in effect, double scales, in that they represent both sines and cosines, the sines increasing from left to right, and the cosines, whose angular values on many rules are marked in red, increasing from right to left. The **S** scale is graduated from left to right for angles from (about) $5°\,44'$ to $90°$, while the **ST** scale is graduated from (about) $0°\,34'$ to $5°\,44'$.

To find the sine of any angle between $5°\,44'$ and $90°$, the left index of **S** is set to the left index of **D**, and under the angle on **S** its sine is read on **D**. It should be borne in mind that the sine of $5°\,44'$ is 0.1, and the sine of $90°$ is 1.0. The sines of angles between $0°\,34'$ and $5°\,44'$ on the **ST** scale are read from the **D** scale, the sine of $0°\,34'$ being 0.01.

Similarly, the cosines of angles between $0°$ and $84°\,16'$, which range downward from 1.0 to 0.1 for $5°\,44'$, are read from the **D** scale below the value of the angle on **S**. The cosines of angles between $84°\,16'$ and $89°\,26'$, which range downward in value from 0.1 to 0.01, are read on the **D** scale below the value of the angle on the **ST** scale.

As its designation indicates, the **ST** scale represents both sines and tangents. The values of sines and tangents of small angles are so nearly equal that the same scale can be used for both, without incurring appreciable error.

Graduation of Angles

Two methods of graduating angles are used on slide rules: one is to graduate them in degrees and minutes of arc, 60 minutes being equal to 1 degree; and the other is to graduate them in degrees and decimals of degrees. Since minutes of arc, rather than decimals of degrees, are customarily used in navigation, this book is based on the assumption that the reader is using a rule graduated in minutes. However, decimals of degrees may be converted to minutes of arc, and vice versa, as explained below. All that is necessary is to remember that 1 degree equals 60 minutes.

For example, to convert 21.°35 to minutes of arc, set 6 on **C** to the right index of **D**, and over 35 on **D** read 21 on **C**. Therefore, 21.°35 equals 21°21′. Again, to convert 0.°86 to minutes, with the rule set as above, over 86 on **D** read 516 on **C**. Therefore, 0.°86 equals 51.′6.

To convert minutes of arc to decimals of a degree, the above procedure is reversed. With 6 on **C** set to the right index of **D**, find the required minutes of arc on **C**, and read the equivalent decimals of a degree below it on **D**. Thus, to convert 43.′7 to decimals of a degree, with 6 on **C** set to the index of **D**, below 43.7 on **C** read 72.8 on **D**. Therefore, 43.′7 equals 0.°728.

T Scale

The **T** scale is marked from left to right to represent angles from 5°43′ to 45°; markings reading from right to left, and usually lettered in red, represent angles from 45° to 84°16′.

When the index of the **T** scale is set to the index of **D**, the tangent of any angle between 5°43′ and 45° will be found on **D** directly below the given angle on **T**, the tangent of 5°43′ being 0.1, and the tangent of 45° being 1.0. *The tangents of angles between 45° and 84°16′ are read from the* **CI** *scale,* the tangent of 45° being 1.0, and that of 84°17′ being 10.0.

The tangent of any angle between 0°34′ and 5°43′, like the sine of such an angle, is read on **D** below the value of the angle on **ST**; the value of tangents in this angular range increases from 0.01 for 0°34′ to 0.1 for 5°43′.

The **ST** scale is also used to find the tangents of angles ranging from 84°17′ to 89°25′; their tangents range from 10 to 100, and are read from the **CI** scale.

To find the tangent of 87°10′, set the hairline to 2°50′ (90° − 87°10′) on **ST**, and under the hairline on **CI** read 202, which would be written 20.2.

The cotangent of a given angle is equal to the tangent of the angle resulting from subtracting the given angle from 90°. Thus, the cotangent of 48° is equal to the tangent of 42° (90° − 48°).

Angles Greater than 90°

Angles greater than 90° pose no real difficulty, since the functions (sines, tangents, and so forth) of an angle greater than 90° are identical to the functions of the angle resulting from subtracting the given angle from 180°. Thus, to find the sine of 109°, subtract 109° from 180°, obtaining 71°. The sine of 71° is 0.946, which is therefore also the sine of 109°.

Sines and Tangents of Small Angles

As we have seen, the **ST** scale is calibrated down to (about) $0°34'$ only; occasionally, we must work with angles smaller than this. On the **ST** scale, there is a gauge point in the vicinity of $1°58'$. To find the sine or tangent of an angle less than (about) $35'$, the gauge point on **ST** is set over the numerical value of the angle on the **D** scale, and the sine or tangent of the angle is read under the gauge point on the **D** scale.

For example, to find the sine or tangent of $0°20'$, set the gauge point over 2 on **D**, and under the index of **ST** read 582; this would be written as 0.00582. Bear in mind that the sines and tangents of angles of $34'$ to $5°44'$ fall in the range of 0.01 to 0.1, while from $34'$ down to $3'.4$ they fall between 0.01 and 0.001.

On some rules, this gauge point appears on the **C** scale in the vicinity of 2.9. With such rules, the procedure is reversed, and the index of **C** is set to the value of the angle in minutes on **D**; the sine of the angle is then read on **D** under the gauge point on **C**.

Plane and Spherical Trigonometry

Functions of Right Plane Triangles

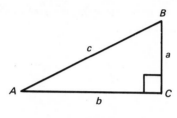

Figure 1

$$\text{Sine (sin) } A = \frac{\text{Side opposite}}{\text{Hypotenuse}} = \frac{a}{c} = \frac{1}{\csc A}$$

$$\text{Cosine (cos) } A = \frac{\text{Side adjacent}}{\text{Hypotenuse}} = \frac{b}{c} = \frac{1}{\sec A}$$

$$\text{Tangent (tan) } A = \frac{\text{Side opposite}}{\text{Side adjacent}} = \frac{a}{b} = \frac{1}{\cot A}$$

$$\text{Cotangent (cot) } A = \frac{\text{Side adjacent}}{\text{Side opposite}} = \frac{b}{a} = \frac{1}{\tan A}$$

$$\text{Secant (sec) } A = \frac{\text{Hypotenuse}}{\text{Side adjacent}} = \frac{c}{b} = \frac{1}{\cos A}$$

$$\text{Cosecant (csc) } A = \frac{\text{Hypotenuse}}{\text{Side opposite}} = \frac{c}{a} = \frac{1}{\sin A}$$

Solutions of Right Triangles

$$a = c \sin A = b \tan A$$

$$b = c \cos A = a \cot A$$

$$c = a \csc A = b \sec A = \frac{a}{\sin A} = \frac{b}{\cos A}$$

Solutions of Oblique Plane Triangles

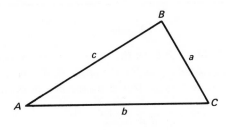

Figure 2

$$A = 180° - (B + C)$$

Law of sines
$$\frac{a}{\sin A} = \frac{b}{\sin B} = \frac{c}{\sin C}$$

Law of cosines
$$a^2 = b^2 + c^2 - 2bc \cos A$$

and
$$\cos A = \frac{b^2 + c^2 - a^2}{2bc}$$

1. Given two sides, b and c, and the included angle A

$$a = \sqrt{b^2 + c^2 - 2bc \cos A}$$

and
$$\sin B = \frac{b}{a} \sin A$$

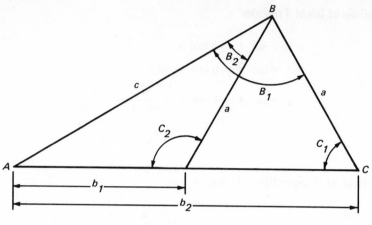

Figure 3

Note: Since B and $180° - B$ have the same sine, the formula immediately above gives two possible solutions for the angle B, B_1 and B_2. If the correct value of B is in doubt, it may be found by the law of cosines

$$\cos B = \frac{a^2 + c^2 - b^2}{2\,ac}$$

2. Given three sides, a, b, and c

$$\cos A = \frac{b^2 + c^2 - a^2}{2\,bc}$$

and
$$\sin C = \frac{c}{a} \sin A$$

Proceed as outlined in the Note above.

3. Given two angles, A and B, and the side b

$$C = 180° - (A + B)$$

$$a = \frac{b \sin A}{\sin B}$$

and
$$c = \frac{b \sin C}{\sin B}$$

4. Given two sides, a and b, and an adjacent angle, A, it is assumed that A is less than 90°. If $c \sin A$ is less than a, and a is less than c, two solutions are possible.

$$\sin C_1 = \frac{c}{a} \sin A$$

$$B_1 = 180° - (A + C_1)$$

$$b_1 = \frac{a \sin B_1}{\sin A}$$

and

$$C_2 = 180° - C_1$$

$$B_2 = 180° - (A + C_2)$$

$$b_2 = \frac{a \sin B_2}{\sin A}$$

See Figure 3.

Some of the formulae for solving oblique plane triangles are given below. By reassigning letters to sides and angles, they can be used to solve for the unknown parts of such triangles.

Known	To find	Formula	Comments
a, b, c	A	$\cos A = \dfrac{c^2 + b^2 - a^2}{2bc}$	Cosine law
a, b, A	B	$\sin B = \dfrac{b \sin A}{a}$	Sine law. Two solutions if $b > a$
	C	$C = 180° - (A + B)$	$A + B + C = 180°$
	c	$c = \dfrac{a \sin C}{\sin A}$	Sine law
a, b, C	A	$\tan A = \dfrac{a \sin C}{b - a \cos C}$	
	B	$B = 180° - (A + C)$	$A + B + C = 180°$
	c	$c = \dfrac{a \sin C}{\sin A}$	Sine law
a, A, B	b	$b = \dfrac{a \sin B}{\sin A}$	Sine law
	C	$C = 180° - (A + B)$	$A + B + C = 180°$
	c	$c = \dfrac{a \sin C}{\sin A}$	Sine law

U.S. Naval Oceanographic Office, H.O. Publication No. 9 (Bowditch).

Area of Triangles
The area of a triangle equals one-half its base multiplied by its perpendicular height.

13

Right Spherical Triangles

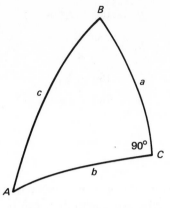

Figure 4

According to "Napier's Rules," the sine of the middle part equals the product of the tangents of the adjacent parts, or the cosines of the opposite parts. Thus,

$$\sin a \ = \tan b \cot B = \sin c \sin A$$

$$\sin b \ = \tan a \cot A = \sin c \sin B$$

$$\cos c \ = \cot A \cot B = \cos a \cos b$$

$$\cos A = \tan b \cot c \ = \cos a \sin B$$

$$\cos B = \tan a \cot c \ = \cos b \sin A$$

In the above equations, the following rules apply:

1. An oblique angle and the side opposite are in the same quadrant.
2. The hypotenuse, c, is less than 90° when a and b are in the same quadrant, and greater than 90° when a and b are in different quadrants.

Oblique Spherical Triangles

An oblique spherical triangle can be solved by dropping a perpendicular from an apex to the opposite side, and, if necessary, extending it to form two right spherical triangles. By reassigning letters as necessary, it can also be solved by the formulae given in the table below. The haversine (hav) is half the versine, which is $1 (-)$ the cosine. Thus, hav $a = \dfrac{1 - \cos a}{2}$.

14

Known	To find	Formula	Comments
a, b, c	A	$\mathrm{hav}\ A = \dfrac{\mathrm{hav}\ a - \mathrm{hav}\ (b-c)}{\sin b \sin c}$	
A, B, C	a	$\mathrm{hav}\ a = \dfrac{-\cos S \cos (S-A)}{\sin B \sin C}$	$S = \frac{1}{2}(A + B + C)$
a, b, C	c	$\mathrm{hav}\ c = \mathrm{hav}\ (a \sim b) + \sin a \sin b\ \mathrm{hav}\ C$	
	A	$\tan A = \dfrac{\sin D \tan C}{\sin (b - D)}$	$\tan D = \tan a \cos C$
	B	$\sin B = \dfrac{\sin C \sin b}{\sin c}$	
c, A, B	C	$\cos C = \sin A \sin B \cos c - \cos A \cos B$	
	a	$\tan a = \dfrac{\tan c \sin E}{\sin (B + E)}$	$\tan E = \tan A \cos c$
	b	$\tan b = \dfrac{\tan c \sin F}{\sin (A + F)}$	$\tan F = \tan B \cos c$
a, b, A	c	$\sin (c + G) = \dfrac{\cos a \sin G}{\cos b}$	$\cot G = \cos A \tan b$ Two solutions
	B	$\sin B = \dfrac{\sin A \sin b}{\sin a}$	Two solutions
	C	$\sin (C + H) = \sin H \tan b \cot a$	$\tan H = \tan A \cos b$ Two solutions
a, A, B	C	$\sin (C - K) = \dfrac{\cos A \sin K}{\cos B}$	$\cot K = \tan B \cos a$ Two solutions
	b	$\sin b = \dfrac{\sin a \sin B}{\sin A}$	Two solutions
	c	$\sin (c - M) = \cot A \tan B \sin M$	$\tan M = \cos B \tan a$ Two solutions

U.S. Naval Oceanographic Office, H.O. Publication No. 9 (Bowditch).

Symbols Used in Navigation

Δ   Delta; difference; unit of change

λ Lambda; longitude

θ Theta; latitude

±   Plus or minus according to appropriate rule

~   Absolute difference, i.e., subtract smaller from larger

∴   Therefore

∵   Because

∞   Infinity

°   Degrees

′   Minutes of arc

″   Seconds of arc

∟   Angle

>   Greater than

<   Less than

☉   Sun

☽   Upper limb Sun

☟   Lower limb Sun

☾   Moon

☽   Upper limb Moon

☟   Lower limb Moon

♀   Venus

♂   Mars

♃   Jupiter

♄   Saturn

♈   Aries

*   Star

Selected Abbreviations Used in Navigation

Note: In the following text, abbreviations are identified as they are used. The following are listed because of the frequency of their use or because of their confusing similarity.

a   Intercept
C   Centigrade, or Celsius, temperature; chronometer time; compass; correction; course; course angle
Cn   Course, referred to true North
DR   Dead reckoning; dead-reckoning position
GP   Geographic position
H   Altitude
ha   Apparent altitude
Hc   Computed altitude
HE   Height of eye
Ho   Fully corrected observed altitude
hs   Sextant altitude
ht   Tabulated altitude
PZM   Navigational triangle, described by the pole, P, the observer's position, Z, and the geographic position of the celestial body, M
Z   Azimuth angle; zenith; upper branch, zone meridian
ZD   Zone description
Zn   Azimuth reckoned from North, as distinguished from azimuth angle

Inshore Navigation

Speed, Time, and Distance

Among the problems most frequently encountered at sea are those involving speed, time, and distance. Having travelled a certain distance in a certain time, what was the speed? Given a certain speed, how long will it take to travel a certain distance? Having spent a certain amount of time travelling at a given speed, what distance was covered? The answers to these questions can be supplied rapidly and accurately by use of the slide rule.

In formulae (1), (2), and (3) below, it is assumed that the time involved is short enough to be conveniently reckoned in minutes. When such is not the case, the factor "60" is dropped and the time is obtained in hours and decimals of hours: to convert the decimals to minutes, multiply them by 60. When seconds are involved, they should be converted to decimals of a minute; that is to say, they should be divided by 60. In most instances, it is acceptable to work to the nearest tenth of a minute. Thus, 47 seconds, which is 0.783 minutes, would ordinarily be written 0.8 minutes.

Also, in formulae (1), (2), and (3), distance is stated in miles and decimals of miles.

To determine speed, when distance and time are known, the formula is

$$\text{Speed} = \frac{\text{distance} \times 60}{\text{time, in minutes}} \tag{1}$$

To determine time, when distance and speed are known, the formula is

$$\text{Time, in minutes} = \frac{\text{distance} \times 60}{\text{speed}} \tag{2}$$

To determine distance, when speed and time are known, the formula is

$$\text{Distance} = \frac{\text{speed} \times \text{time, in minutes}}{60} \tag{3}$$

From time to time, it is necessary to determine speed over the measured mile. In this instance, the time is taken in seconds, and the formula is

$$\text{Speed} = \frac{3600}{\text{time, in seconds}} \tag{4}$$

The following examples illustrate the use of these formulae.

Example 1: We have covered 9.6 miles in 32 minutes and 24 seconds, which equals 32.4 minutes, and want to determine our speed. Formula (1) becomes

$$\text{Speed} = \frac{9.6 \text{ miles} \times 60}{32.4 \text{ minutes}} = 17.8$$

Our speed, therefore, is 17.8 knots.

Example 2: Our speed is 12.25 knots, and we want to know how many minutes and seconds will be required to travel 11.4 miles. Formula (2) becomes

$$\text{Time} = \frac{11.4 \text{ miles} \times 60}{12.25 \text{ knots}} = 55.8$$

The time required will, therefore, be 55.8 minutes, or 55 minutes and 48 seconds.

Example 3: We are steaming at 12 knots, and wish to know how far we travelled in 43 minutes. Formula (3) becomes

$$\text{Distance} = \frac{12 \text{ knots} \times 43 \text{ minutes}}{60} = 8.6$$

We have, therefore, steamed 8.6 nautical miles in 43 minutes.

Example 4: We steamed the measured mile in 4 minutes and 5 seconds, which equals 245 seconds, and wish to determine our speed in knots. Formula (4) becomes

$$\text{Speed} = \frac{3600}{245 \text{ seconds}} = 14.7$$

Our speed, therefore, is 14.7 knots.

Example 5: The next leg of our voyage is 89.5 miles, we are steaming at 15.6 knots, and we wish to know how long it will take to traverse the next leg. Here we will use Formula (2), omitting the factor 60, as the time obviously will run into hours

$$\text{Time, in hours} = \frac{89.5}{15.6} = 5.74$$

The time required, therefore, will be 5.74 hours, which equals 5 hours and 44.4 minutes, or 5 hours, 44 minutes, and 24 seconds. Since time is ordinarily stated to the nearest minute, the answer would be written 5 hours and 44 minutes.

Distance to the Horizon

Because of the Earth's curvature, the distance to the sea horizon increases as the height of the observer's eye increases. Also, for any given height of eye, the distance increases because of terrestrial refraction, or the bending of the light rays caused by the atmosphere.

Knowing the distance to the horizon for your height of eye can be very helpful in estimating distances at sea. For example, when you sight an approaching steamer hull down, that knowledge allows you to determine the range with fair accuracy when her bow wave appears.

The formulae for determining the distance to the horizon for a given height of eye include a correction for terrestrial refraction calculated for normal atmospheric conditions.

For the distance in *nautical miles,* the formula is

$$D_1 = 1.144 \sqrt{HE} \tag{1}$$

and for *statute miles* it is

$$D_2 = 1.317 \sqrt{HE} \tag{2}$$

where D is the distance, and HE is the height, in feet, of the observer's eye above the surface.

Example: Your height of eye is 17 feet. What is the distance, in nautical miles, to the horizon?

$$D_1 = 1.144 \sqrt{17}, \text{ or } 4.72$$

The distance to the horizon is, therefore, 4.72 nautical miles.

Distance by Sextant Angle

Distance by Horizon Angle

The distance to an object located between the horizon and the viewer may be determined by use of the angle subtended between the horizon and the object's waterline, as measured by sextant. To this angle, corrected for sextant index error, is applied the correction for the dip of the horizon for the observer's height of eye with the *sign reversed;* that is to say, the dip correction is added to the sextant angle. The sextant angle, thus corrected, is termed the horizon angle, H.

The distance, D, may now be found by the formula

$$D = \frac{HE}{\sin H} \times \cos H \tag{1}$$

where HE is the height of the observer's eye above water. Both D and HE are measured in feet. In the great majority of instances, when distance is being found by this method, H is less than $5°$. When such is the case, in working with the slide rule, $\cos H$ may be considered as unity.

If the distance is to be given in yards, the formula becomes

$$D, \text{ in yards} = \frac{HE}{\sin H} \times \frac{\cos H}{3} \tag{2}$$

The greater the height of eye, the greater the accuracy obtained at shorter ranges, and the greater the ranges that can be obtained.

Example 1: The angle subtended between the horizon and the waterline of a buoy is $1°05.'2$, the sextant's index error is $-2.'5$, and the observer's height of eye is 20 feet. What is the distance, in feet, between the buoy and the observer?

The first step is to determine the horizon angle, *H*, and the formula for doing so is

Sextant angle		1°05.′2
Index correction	+ 2.′5	
Dip for 20 feet, sign reversed,	+ 4.′3	
	+ 6.′8	+ 6.′8
		H 1°12.′0

If a dip table is not available, the dip may be calculated by the formula for finding the dip of the horizon, given on page 68.

H being less than 5°, Formula (1) becomes

$$D = \frac{20}{\sin 1°\,12.′0} \times 1$$

and $$D = 955$$

The distance to the buoy is, therefore, 955 feet.

Example 2: The height of eye is 95 feet, and the angle between the water-line of a boat and the horizon behind it, as measured by sextant, is 0°11.′3. The sextant is without index error. We need the range, in yards, to the boat.

We first determine *H*, as follows

Sextant angle		0°11.′3
Index correction	0′	
Dip for 95 feet, sign reversed,	+ 9.′5	
Net correction		+ 9.′5
		H 0°20.′8

Since the range is to be given in yards, we use Formula (2), and it becomes

$$D = \frac{95}{\sin 20.′8} \times \frac{1}{3}$$

Before we can proceed, we must determine the value of sin 20.′8, and this is done by setting the "minutes" mark, (′), on the **ST** scale to 20.8 on the **D** scale, and reading .00605 on the **D** scale, under the index of **ST**.

The formula then becomes

$$D = \frac{95}{.00605} \times \frac{1}{3} = 5,235$$

The range to the boat, therefore, is 5,235 yards.

Distance Short of Horizon

The sextant may be used as an accurate range finder when the height of an object is known, and when its base at the water, or waterline, does not lie beyond the observer's horizon. When the angle between top and base, measured by sextant, is less than about 10°, as it is in the majority of cases, we may assume for practical purposes that the distance to the top of the object and that to its waterline are the same. The index correction must, of course, always be applied to the sextant angle.

When the height of an object, such as the top of a lighthouse above the waterline, or the truck of a mast above the boot top or waterline, is known in feet, the distance, D, in thousands of feet, may be found by the formula

$$D, \text{ in feet } = \frac{A}{\sin H} \tag{1}$$

where A is the height of the object in feet, and H is the corrected sextant angle.

The left-hand index of the **ST** scale is at about 34.'38. The sines and tangents of angles smaller than 34.'38 may be found under the index of the **S** scale when the minute mark, ('), which on most rules is at about 1° 58' on the **ST** scale, is set to the value of the angle on the **D** scale. Remember that, whereas sines and tangents in the range between about 5° 44.'4 and 34.'38, are read in hundredths, those between 34.'38 and 3.'44 are read in thousandths. Thus, sin 15' is .00436.

If the distance is desired in yards, it is necessary only to divide the answer by three.

Example 1: The top of the light on a lighthouse is 224 feet above the water. The corrected angle between the water and the top of the light is found by sextant to be 29.'5. We require the distance, in yards, to the light. Formula (1) becomes

$$D = \frac{224 \text{ feet}}{\sin 29.'5 \times 3} = \frac{224}{.00858 \times 3} = 8{,}700$$

The distance, therefore, is 8,700 yards.

The factor for converting feet to nautical miles is 0.0001645. Therefore, if the distance is to be determined in nautical miles, the formula becomes

$$D, \text{ in nautical miles } = \frac{A \text{ in feet} \times 0.0001645}{\sin H} \tag{2}$$

27

Should the distance be required in statute miles, the factor would be 0.0001892.

Example 2: An object is known to be 183 feet above the water. The corrected sextant angle between its top and the waterline is 1°13.'5. What is the distance in nautical miles?

Formula (2) becomes

$$D, \text{ in nautical miles} = \frac{183 \text{ feet} \times 0.0001645}{\sin 1°13.'5} = 1.41$$

The distance, therefore, is 1.41 nautical miles.

Example 3: An object is known to be 247 feet high. The height, as measured by sextant, is 1°50.'8. What is the distance in statute miles?

Formula (2) becomes

$$D, \text{ in statute miles} = \frac{247 \text{ feet} \times 0.0001892}{\sin 1°50.'8} = 1.45$$

The distance, therefore, is 1.45 statute miles.

Distance in nautical miles may also be determined by sextant angle using only the **C** and **D** scales. In this case, the height, in feet, of the observed object is divided by the sextant altitude *in minutes,* and the result is multiplied by 0.566. The formula, therefore, is

$$D, \text{ in nautical miles} = \frac{\text{height of object, in feet} \times 0.566}{\text{sextant angle, in minutes}} \tag{3}$$

Example 4: Using the same data as in Example 2, a height of 183 feet, and a corrected sextant angle of 1°13.'5,

Formula (3) becomes

$$D, \text{ in nautical miles} = \frac{183 \text{ feet} \times 0.566}{73.'5} = 1.41$$

The distance, therefore, is 1.41 nautical miles.

Some years ago, a defender in the America's Cup races used this method to keep a regular check on the range between himself and his challenger, whose mast height he knew. He had, of course, to allow for the challenger's angle of heel, so that the actual height of the mast above the water could be used. Since his boat and the challenger were about equally stiff, he assumed that the challenger's angle of heel was the same as his own.

He then determined the current height of his challenger's mast truck above the water by multiplying vertical mast height by the cosine of the angle of the heel, and used this height, in conjunction with Formula (1), above, to determine the range.

Distance Beyond Horizon

In clear weather, an object such as a mountain, can be seen even when it is well beyond the horizon. If its height is known, its approximate distance can be determined with a sextant.

The first step is to correct the sextant altitude for any index error, for the dip of the horizon (height-of-eye correction), and for refraction. *For this purpose,* refraction is found by dividing the estimated distance in nautical miles by 13.75: it is obtained in minutes and tenths of minutes of arc, and subtracted from the sextant altitude.

Next, correction must be made for the curvature of the Earth. This is done by multiplying the square of the estimated distance in nautical miles by 0.907; the product, which is in feet, has to be subtracted from the height of the object. The corrected height is then divided by the corrected sextant altitude, stated in minutes of arc, and the quotient is multiplied by the factor 0.566 to obtain the distance in nautical miles.

When the distance thus found varies considerably from the estimated distance used in obtaining the refraction and in correcting for the curvature of the Earth, the problem should be reworked, using the distance found as the estimated distance.

Example: The sextant altitude of a 7,000-foot mountain, estimated to be 38 miles distant, is $1°25.'5$. The height of eye is 45 feet, and the sextant has no index error. To determine as closely as possible its actual distance, we set up the problem in the following form

Alt by sextant		$1°25.'5$	Height of mountain	7,000 ft
Dip (45 feet)	$-6.'5$		Correct. for curvature	
Refraction			Est distance 38.0,	
$\left(\dfrac{38}{13.75}\right)$	$-2.'8$		squared $\times$ 0.907	$-1,310$ ft
Net correction	$-9.'3$			

$$-9.'3$$
$$1°16.'2 = 76.'2 \quad \text{Corrected height} \quad 5,690 \text{ ft}$$

$$\text{Corrected height} \quad \frac{5,690}{76.'2} \times 0.566 = 42.3$$

Corrected sextant altitude, in minutes

29

The mountain, therefore, appears to be 42.3 miles distant.

Since estimated distance was 4.3 miles less than the solution obtained, the problem should be reworked, using 42.3 miles as the estimated distance. Thus

Alt by sextant	1° 25.′5	Height of mountain	7,000 ft
Dip	−6.′5	Est distance 42.3	
Refraction		squared × 0.907	−1,620 ft

$\left(\dfrac{42.3}{13.75}\right)$ −3.′1

Net correction   −9.′6

−9.′6

1° 15.′9 = 75.′9   Corrected height   5,380 ft

Corrected height   5,380

Corrected sextant altitude, in minutes $\dfrac{5{,}380}{75.′9}$ × 0.566 = 40.1

The distance to the mountain now appears to be 40.1 miles and, if no considerable anomaly exists in the refraction, this is in all probability correct to within about one mile.

Distance of Visibility of Objects

When the height of an object is known, it is simple to determine the distance at which, under normal atmospheric conditions, it should become visible for a given height of eye. All that is required is to solve the distance to the horizon for the observer's height of eye, and the distance to the horizon for the height of the object, and add the results.

The formulae used are those given for calculating distance to the horizon, where D represents distance and HE represents height of eye, in feet

$$D_1, \text{ in nautical miles} = 1.144\sqrt{HE} \tag{1}$$

$$D_2, \text{ in statute miles} = 1.317\sqrt{HE} \tag{2}$$

Example 1: Your height of eye is 63 feet, and the height of a brilliant light is 178 feet. At what distance, in nautical miles, should the light become visible?

Formula (1) becomes

$$D_1 = 1.144\sqrt{63} = 9.08$$
$$D_1 = 1.144\sqrt{178} = {}^{+}\ 15.26$$
$$\overline{ 24.34}$$

Under normal atmospheric conditions, therefore, you would expect to pick up the light at a distance of 24.3 nautical miles.

Example 2: Your height of eye is 6 feet, and the height of the brilliant light is 97 feet. At what distance, in statute miles, should the light become visible?

Formula (2) becomes

$$
\begin{aligned}
D_2 &= 1.317\sqrt{6} = \\
D_2 &= 1.317\sqrt{97} =
\end{aligned}
\quad + \quad
\begin{aligned}
3.23 \\
\underline{12.97} \\
16.20
\end{aligned}
$$

Under normal atmospheric conditions, therefore, you would expect to see the light at a distance of 16.2 statute miles.

Distance by Bearings

Distance Off Abeam by One Bearing and Run to Beam

The distance off when abeam of a fixed object can be determined by taking a bearing on the bow, and noting the distance run from the time of that bearing to the time the object is abeam. Solution is by the law of sines

$$D = \frac{R \times \sin A}{\cos A}$$

where D is the distance off when abeam, R is the run, and A is the angle on the bow.

Example: We pick up a light bearing 319° relative, and after we have run 6.0 miles, it is abeam. We wish to know the distance off when the light was abeam.

Since 319° relative is 41° on the bow, the formula becomes

$$D = \frac{6.0 \times \sin 41°}{\cos 41°} = 5.22$$

We were, therefore, 5.2 miles off the light when it was abeam.

Distance Off at Second Bearing by Two Bearings on Bow and Run Between

The distance from a fixed object can readily be determined by two bearings on the bow, if the ship's run between the bearings is known. Best results are obtained when the change in bearing is considerable.

Solution is by the law of sines

$$D = \frac{R \times \sin A}{\sin (A \sim B)}$$

where D is the distance off at the time of the second bearing, A is the first bearing on the bow, B the second bearing on the bow, and R the run between bearings.

Example 1: A landmark bears $20°$ on the bow. After steaming 5.0 miles, the mark bears $70°$ on the bow. We require the distance off at the time of the second bearing.

The formula, becomes

$$D = \frac{5.0 \times \sin 20°}{\sin (20° \sim 70°)} = \frac{5.0 \times \sin 20°}{\sin 50°} = 2.23$$

At the time of the second bearing, therefore, our distance from the mark was 2.23 miles.

Example 2: We are on course $323°$ True, and obtain a bearing of $347°$ True on a light. After steaming 8.0 miles the light bears $016°$ True. We require the distance off the light at the time of the second bearing.

The first bearing is $24°(347° - 323°)$ on the bow, and the second is $53°(376° - 323°)$. The formula becomes

$$D = \frac{8.0 \times \sin 24°}{\sin 29°} = 6.7$$

The light was, therefore, 6.7 miles distant at the time of the second bearing.

Distance Off When Abeam by Two Bearings on the Bow and Run Between

The distance off a fixed object when abeam can be determined from two bearings on the bow, and the run between them. Here, again, solution is by the law of sines.

In this case, the first step is to determine the distance between the ship and the object, at the time of the first bearing. This can be done when the second bearing is obtained by determining the angle at the object formed by the two bearing lines, and considering this angle to be the apex of a triangle. For example, if the first bearing were $30°$ on the bow, and the second were $50°$, the angle at the object would be $20°$ $[180° - (130° + 30°)]$. The distance off the object at the time of the first bearing is then found by the formula

$$D_1 = \frac{R \times \sin B_2}{\sin C} \tag{1}$$

where D_1 is the distance off at the first bearing, R is the run between the first and second bearing, B_2 the second bearing on the bow, and C the angle between the two bearing lines at the object.

Having solved that equation, the distance off the object when it is abeam is found by the formula

$$D_2 = \frac{D_1 \times \sin A}{\sin 90°} \tag{2}$$

or $\qquad D_2 = D_1 \times \sin A$, $\sin 90°$ being equal to 1

where A is the first angle on the bow, D_1 the distance off the object at the time of the first bearing, and D_2 the distance off when the object is abeam.

Example: We sight a light bearing 28° on the bow. After steaming 6.5 miles, it bears 52° on the bow. We wish to know the distance off the light when it is abeam.

First, we determine the angle at the light, C in Formula (1) above, and to do so, we subtract the first bearing, 28°, from the second, 52°; and we get 24°. Formula (1) becomes

$$D_1 = \frac{6.5 \times \sin 52°}{\sin 24°} = 12.6$$

Formula (2) then becomes

$$D_2 = 12.6 \times \sin 28° = 5.92$$

The light will, therefore, be distant 5.9 miles when it is abeam.

Run to a Given Bearing and Distance Off When on That Bearing

It is at times necessary to determine the distance to steam to bring a fixed object to a given bearing, and the distance off the object when it is on that bearing. The problem is illustrated in Figure 5.

Two bearings on the bow are obtained, and the run between them is noted. The distance off at the time the first bearing was obtained can then be determined by the formula

$$D_1 = \frac{R_1 \times \sin B}{\sin C} \tag{1}$$

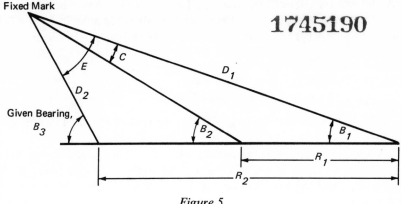

Figure 5

D_1 being the distance off at the first bearing, R_1 the run between the first and second bearing, B the second bearing on the bow, and C the angle between the two bearing lines at the object.

Having found the distance off the object at the time of the first bearing, the distance to steam to bring the object to the given or second bearing is calculated by the formula

$$R_2 = \frac{D_1 \times \sin E}{\sin F} \tag{2}$$

R_2 being the run from the first bearing to the given bearing, D_1 the distance off the object at the first bearing, E the angle at the object formed by the first bearing line and the bearing of the object when on the given bearing, and F the bearing on the bow of the object when on the given bearing.

The distance off the object at the time of the given bearing, D_2, is found by the formula

$$D_2 = \frac{D_1 \times \sin A}{\sin F} \tag{3}$$

A being the first bearing on the bow.

Example: We are steaming on course 273°, speed 12.0 knots, when a navigational light on shore comes into sight. Course is to be altered to 305° when the light bears 333° per gyro compass. At 2207 the light bears 293° per gyro, at 2257 it bears 308°. At what time will the course be changed, and how far will we be off the light at that time?

As we are on course 273°, the first bearing is 20° on the bow, and the second is 35°; at 12.0 knots, we have steamed exactly 10 miles in 50 minutes. The angle at the light formed by our two bearing lines is 15°. Formula (1) becomes

$$D_1 = \frac{10.0 \times \sin 35°}{\sin 15°} = 22.15$$

At the time of the first bearing, 2207, we were, therefore, 22.15 miles from the light.

The course change is to take effect when the light bears 333° per gyro. The bearing on the bow will then be 60°; the angle at the light between this bearing line and the first bearing line is therefore 40° (60° − 20°). Formula (2) becomes

$$R_2 = \frac{22.15 \times \sin 40°}{\sin 60°} = 16.425$$

so the run from the first bearing to the turning bearing is 16.4 miles. The time of the first bearing was 2207; at 12.0 knots, it will take us 82 minutes to steam 16.4 miles. We can, therefore, expect to change course at 2329. Formula (3) becomes

$$D_2 = \frac{22.15 \times \sin 20°}{\sin 60°} = 8.74$$

We will, therefore, be 8.7 miles off the light when course is changed.

Distance Off Two Landmarks or Seamarks

When the distance between two fixed marks and the bearing of one from the other are known, a vessel's distance from each mark can be determined, without plotting, by true bearings taken on each mark. The problem is illustrated in Figure 6.

Solution is by the law of sines

$$\frac{s}{\sin \lfloor S} : \frac{a}{\sin \lfloor A} : \frac{b}{\sin \lfloor B}$$

In this ratio, $\lfloor A$ represents the angular difference between the true bearing of A from the ship and the bearing of B from A; $\lfloor B$ represents the angular difference between its bearing from A and its true bearing from the ship.

The ship is located at *S*. ⌞*S* represents the angular difference between the true bearings of *A* and *B*. The known distance from *A* to *B* is represented by *s*. The distance of the ship from *A* is represented by *b*, while the distance of the ship from *B* is represented by *a*.

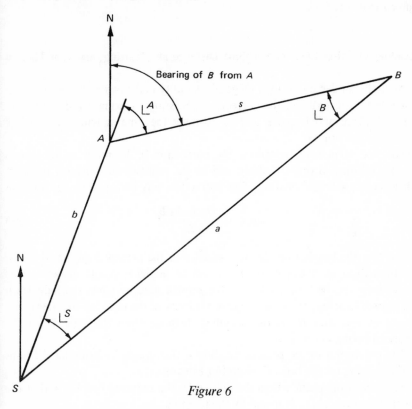

N

Bearing of *B* from *A*

⌞*A*

s

⌞*B*

A

B

b

a

N

⌞*S*

S

Figure 6

Example: Cuttyhunk Light bears 074° True from Buzzards Light, and is distant 3.96 miles. We obtain a bearing of 015° True on Buzzards, which we will call *A*, and of 050° on Cuttyhunk, which we will call *B*. We wish to determine our distance from both lights.

In this case, the angle *S* is 35° (050° − 015°), while the side *s* is 3.96 miles. For the angle *A*, we will use 59° (074° − 015°), and for the angle *B* 24° (074° − 050°). Our distance off Buzzards Light is represented by *b*, and our distance off Cuttyhunk Light by *a*. The ratio becomes

$$\frac{3.96}{\sin 35°} = \frac{a}{\sin 59°} = \frac{b}{\sin 24°}$$

or
$$\frac{3.96}{\sin 35°} = \frac{5.92}{\sin 59°} = \frac{2.81}{\sin 24°}$$

The distance off Buzzards Light, therefore, is 2.81 miles, and off Cutty-hunk Light it is 5.92 miles.

Heading to Bring Light to Specified Distance and Bearing, and Run Thereto

At night, under conditions of good visibility and normal refraction, it is possible to approximate the correction necessary to bring a light to a specified distance and bearing, and to estimate the time at which a ship will arrive at that point.

The first step is to determine the correction to be made to the ship's present heading in order that she will be the requisite distance off the light when on the specified bearing. This correction may be found by the formula

$$\sin C = \frac{D_2 \times \sin B}{D_1} \qquad (1)$$

where C is the bearing on the bow relative to the present heading to which the light must be brought so that it will be at the requisite distance, B is the bearing on the bow relative to the *present heading* when the light is on the desired bearing. D_1 is the range of visibility of the light for the observer's height of eye, and D_2 is the specified distance from the light when the desired bearing is reached.

The correction to the present heading is then made by bringing the light to the bearing on the bow, C, found in Formula (1).

The run to the point where the light is on the required bearing and at the specified distance, D_3, is found by the formula

$$D_3 = \frac{\sin E \times D_1}{\sin F} \qquad (2)$$

E being the angle at the light between the line of the first bearing and the bearing when at the specified distance, and F the light's bearing on the bow relative to the corrected heading when at the specified distance.

Example: We are on course 140°, speed 13.0 knots. Our course is to be changed when Light X is distant 9.0 miles, and bears 205°. For our height of eye, Light X will become visible at a range of 18.6 miles. At 2217 we sight Light X, bearing 160° T, or 20° on the bow.

We wish to determine approximately the change that must be made to our present heading to bring us to the required distance off the light when it bears 205°, and to determine at about what time we will arrive at that point.

Our first step is to find out what the relative bearing of the light should be, when the ship is headed for the point where the course is to be changed. Here, the angle B will be 65° (205° − 140°). Therefore Formula (1) becomes

$$\sin C = \frac{9.0 \times \sin 65°}{18.6} = 0.439, \text{ or } 26°$$

To bring the ship to the point where her course is to be changed, the light should bear 26° on the bow, so we come left 6° to 134°.

We can now find the run to the turning point, using Formula (2), in which E will be 45° (205° − 160°), and F will be 71° (205° − 134°)

$$D_3 = \frac{\sin 45° \times 18.6}{\sin 71°} = 13.9$$

The distance from where the light first came into view to the point where the course is to be changed is, therefore, 13.9 miles. At 13.0 knots, it will take us 64.2 minutes to get there, so we will come to the new course at 2321.

In fact, we should have come left 7.°5 to 133.°5. The actual distance to the turning point would then have been 13.75 miles, and we would have arrived there at 2320. Steering 134°, we would have been 8.68 miles off the light when it bore 205°.

Current Sailing

Course and Speed Made Good for Known Set and Drift

When a current of known set and drift is flowing, the course that a ship must steer in order to offset it, as well as the speed that will be made good over the ground, may readily be determined with a slide rule. Using the law of sines, both the correction angle, that is, the angle between the desired track and the heading to be used to make good that track, and the speed that will be made good over the bottom may be determined by a single setting of the rule.

The solution is as follows: set the angle between the desired track and the set, or direction, of the current (or the supplement of the current's set, if the current is foul or from forward of the beam) on the **S** scale over the ship's speed on the **D** scale. Then over the current's drift on **D** read the correction angle on the **ST** scale, and apply it to the desired track to determine the course that should be steered. If the current is fair, that is, abaft the beam, add this correction angle to the angle between the set and track; conversely, if the current is foul subtract it. Below the angle thus found on the **S** scale, read on the **D** scale the speed made good over the bottom.

Example 1: The current is setting 248°, and the drift is 1.5 knots. We wish to make good a track of 289°, and will steam at 11.0 knots. What should be our heading, and what will be our speed over the bottom?

In this case, the current is fair, so we use the angle between the desired track and the set, 41° (289° − 248°). We set 41° on **S** above the speed, 11.0, on **D**, and above the drift, 1.5, on **D** we read the correction angle, 5° 08′, on **ST**. For practical purposes, we will call the correction angle 5°. The current being on our starboard quarter, we will, therefore, steer 5° to the right of the desired track, making our course 294°. Since the current is fair, we add this correction angle to the angle between the set and the track, and get 46° (5° + 41°). Now, under 46° on **S**, we read 12.05 on **D**, which is our speed over the bottom, and will be called 12.0 knots.

Our heading, therefore, should be 294°, and our speed over the bottom will be 12.0 knots.

Example 2: We wish to make good a track of 160°, and are steaming at 12.0 knots. The current is setting 015°, with a drift of 2.0 knots. What course should we steer, and what speed will we make over the bottom?

The angle between the desired track and the set is 145° (160° − 15°). We use its supplement, 35°, which we set on **S** over 12.0 on **D**, and over 2.0 on **D** we read 5° 30′ on **ST**. The correction angle is, therefore, 5.°5, and as the current is on our starboard bow, the heading to steer will be 165.°5. The supplement of the angle between the desired track and the set is 35°. The current is foul, so we subtract 5.°5 from 35°, and obtain 29.°5. Below 29° 30′ on **S**, we read 10.3 on **D**.

Our course, therefore, should be 165.°5, and we will make 10.3 knots over the ground.

Set and Drift from Track Between Fixes

Sometimes a vessel unexpectedly passes into an area where the current drift is strong, and finds that she is being badly set. The problem here is to determine the set and drift of the current, in order that corrective action may be taken.

In determining the set and drift, departure must be taken from a fixed or known position, and a second fix must be obtained. When the second fix is plotted on a chart, the current vector is represented by a line drawn from the DR position for the time of the second fix, to that fix. Alternatively, unless the distance travelled between fixes is great, it may be found by a plane sailing solution, using the slide rule. If the distance is great, the current vector should be found by mid-latitude sailing. It must be borne in mind that when a considerable amount of time has elapsed between obtaining fixes, the current may not have been flowing during the whole period. In this case, the current is stronger than is indicated in the solution.

Example: We are on course 340°, speed 10.6 knots, headed for the sea buoy at the entrance to the main ship channel at Key West. At 2200, we get a good radar fix which puts us in L 24° 13.′1 N, λ 81° 42.′2 W. At 2300 we obtain another radar fix which puts us in 24° 24.′1 N, λ 81° 43.′0 W.

We wish to determine the set and drift of the current.

We first determine what our 2300 position would have been, if no current had existed. Using 20° for course (360° − 340°), by plane sailing formula the difference of latitude is 9.96 miles North, which we call 10.0 miles, and the departure is 3.625 miles West, which converts to 3.′98 of longitude and which we call 4.′0. At 2300, therefore, our DR latitude is 24°23.′1 N (24°13.′1 + 10.′0) and our DR longitude is 81°46.′2 W (81°42.′2 + 4.′0).

We now compare our 2300 fix with our 2300 DR

Fix	L 24°24.′1 N	81°43.′0 W
DR	L 24°23.′1 N	81°46.′2 W
Difference	1.′0 N	2.′8 E

A difference of 2.′8 of longitude in L 24°24′ is equal to a departure of 2.55 miles. Consequently, in one hour, the current has set us 1.0 miles to the North, and 2.55 miles to the East of our DR position. The set is therefore North and East.

Dividing 1.0 by 2.55 gives 0.392, which is the tangent of 21°25′; we will call it N 21°30′ E. The set, therefore, is 068.°5 (90° − 21.°5) and, by the law of sines, the drift is 2.73 which we will call 2.75 knots.

Direction and Speed of
True Wind

Given the course and speed of a ship, and the direction and speed of the relative wind, the direction and speed of the true wind may be found by solving a vector triangle. The form this triangle takes depends upon whether the apparent wind is from forward of the beam (*see* Figure 7), or from abaft the beam (*see* Figure 8).

In both these triangles, side *a* represents the speed of the true wind and its direction relative to the ship's heading; side *b* represents the speed of the apparent wind and the direction in which it is moving relative to the ship; side *c* represents the speed and course of the ship. In Figure 7, the ship's travel vector is in the direction *AB*, and in Figure 8 it is in the direction *BA*.

The speed of the true wind is found by means of the formula

$$a = \sqrt{b^2 + c^2 \pm 2\,bc \cos A} \tag{1}$$

in which *A* is the angle of the apparent wind relative to the ship's heading, and the sign is $(-)$ if the apparent wind is forward of the beam, and $(+)$ if it is abaft the beam.

Having obtained the speed of the true wind, the next step is to determine its direction relative to the ship's head. This is done by determining the angle *B*; with the wind forward of the beam, the supplement of *B* is used. The formula is

$$\sin B = \frac{b}{a} \sin A \tag{2}$$

All that remains is to apply the angle *B* to the ship's heading.

Example 1: We are on course 090°, speed 12.0 knots, and the apparent wind is blowing from 120° True, speed 25.0 knots. Relative to our heading, 120° True is 030°. We require the speed and direction of the true wind.

43

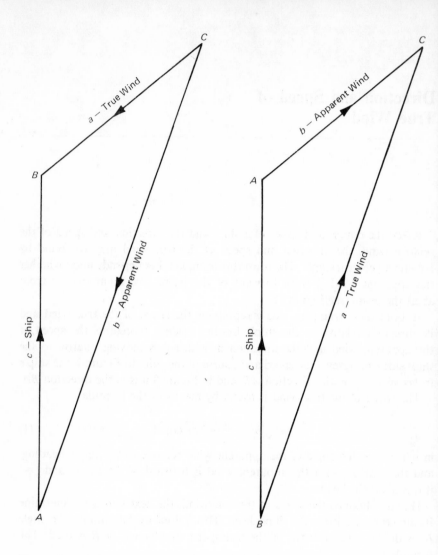

Figure 7

Apparent Wind Forward of the Beam.
Ship's Travel Vector is AB.

Figure 8

Apparent Wind Abaft the Beam.
Ship's Travel Vector is BA.

The apparent wind being forward of the beam, we use the (−) sign and Formula (1) becomes

$$a = \sqrt{25^2 + 12^2 - (2 \times 25 \times 12 \times \cos 30°)}$$
$$= \sqrt{625 + 144 - (600 \times 0.866)}$$
$$= \sqrt{769 - 520}$$
$$= \sqrt{249}$$
$$= 15.8$$

Although we will use 15.8 for a in solving the next formula, the true wind speed is, for practical purposes, stated as 16.0 knots.

To determine the direction of the true wind, we use Formula (2), which becomes

$$\sin B = \frac{25}{15.8} \times \sin 30° = 0.791 = 52°\,20'$$

Here, for practical purposes, we would write 52° 20′ as 52°.

Therefore, 52° represents the supplement of the angle B in Figure 7. Since the apparent wind is on our starboard bow, we add 52° to the ship's heading, and obtain 142° as the true direction from which the wind is blowing.

The true wind, therefore, is at 16.0 knots, from 142°.

Example 2: Our course is 305°, speed 15.0 knots, and the apparent wind is from 230° relative, speed 8.0 knots. What are the speed and direction of the true wind?

In this case the wind is fair, so Formula (1) becomes

$$a = \sqrt{64 + 225 + 2 \times 8 \times 15 \times \cos 50°}$$
$$= \sqrt{289 + 240 \cos 50°}$$
$$= \sqrt{289 + 154}$$
$$= \sqrt{443}$$
$$= 21.05$$

The speed of the true wind, therefore, is 21.05 knots.

To obtain the direction of the true wind, Formula (2) becomes

$$\sin B = \frac{8}{21.05} \times \sin 50° = .291 = 16°\,55'$$

The true wind, therefore, is from 197° (180° + 17°) relative to our ship's heading, or from 142° True, and its speed, to the nearest knot, is 21.0 knots.

Great-Circle Direction Converted to Mercator Direction, and Vice Versa

Aboard ship, it is frequently necessary to convert a great-circle bearing, or direction, to a rhumb line, which is its equivalent Mercator value, so that it can be plotted on a Mercator chart. This problem most frequently involves radio-direction-finder bearings, which, of course, are great-circle bearings, and it can be solved by determining the conversion angle. Conversely, given a Mercator bearing, the conversion angle permits determination of the equivalent great-circle bearing.

Where the difference of longitude between the two points involved, DLo, is less than 5°, the conversion angle may be found by means of the formula

$$\tan \text{ conversion angle} = \sin Lm \times \tan \frac{DLo}{2}$$

in which Lm is the mid latitude.

In determining the sign of the conversion angle, it must be remembered that the great circle lies towards the elevated pole from the rhumb line. Alternatively, the sign may be taken from the table below.

Radio Bearings			Great-Circle Sailing		
Latitude of receiver	*Radio beacon lies to*	*Correction sign*	*Latitude of departure*	*Destination lies to*	*Correction sign*
N	Eastward	+	N	Eastward	−
N	Westward	−	N	Westward	+
S	Eastward	−	S	Eastward	+
S	Westward	+	S	Westward	−

Where the difference of longitude exceeds 5°, one of the formulae given in the section on great-circle sailing should be used to determine the great-circle direction.

Example 1: Our DR position is L 35° 51.′0 N, λ 84° 25.′0 W when we receive a radio bearing of 128.°0 from a beacon located at L 32° 47.′0 N, λ 79° 55.′0 W. In order to plot a line of position on a Mercator chart, we need the conversion angle and its sign.

We tabulate the data

	L	λ	
Ship	35° 51.′0 N	84° 25.′0 W	
Beacon	32° 47.′0 N	79° 55.′0 W	
Difference	3° 04.′0	4° 30.′0	Half difference = 2° 15.′0
Lm	34° 19.′0 N		

With the above data, the formula above becomes

$$\text{tan conversion angle} = \sin 34° 19.′0 \times \tan 2° 15.′0 = 0.0221$$

The conversion angle, therefore, is 1° 16.′0, or 1.°3, and the sign is (+). Thus, the Mercator bearing is 129.°3 (128.°0 + 1.°3).

Example 2: We are in L 47° 19.′0 N, λ 49° 23.′6 W, and wish to determine the great-circle bearing of Point A, located in L 51° 47.′5 N, λ 53° 31.′7 W. From a Mercator chart, Point A bears 329.°0.

We tabulate the data, as in Example 1

	L	λ	
Ship	47° 19.′0 N	49° 23.′6 W	
Point A	51° 47.′5 N	53° 31.′7 W	
Difference	4° 28.′5	4° 08.′1	Half difference = 2° 04.′0
Lm	49° 33.′3 N		

and write the formula

$$\text{tan conversion angle} = \sin 49° 33.′3 \times \tan 2° 04.′0 = 0.0274$$

The conversion angle, therefore, equals 1° 34.′5, or, for our purpose, 1.°6. In this case we are converting a rhumb-line bearing to a great-circle bearing, we are in North latitude, and Point A lies to the westward. Therefore, the sign of the conversion angle is (+), and the great-circle bearing is 330.°6 (329.°0 + 1.°6).

Consolan and Consol

Consolan and Consol are names for similar systems of electronic navigation. The system used in the United States is called Consolan, and the one in wide use in Europe is called Consol.

A Consolan signal frequently provides an excellent line of position, LOP, at ranges up to about 1,500 miles from the transmitter. When a Consolan chart is available and the DR position is reasonably accurate, no problem is encountered in plotting an LOP.

Consolan bearing tables enable the signals, which give true bearings, to be plotted on a Mercator chart, even when the area covered by the chart does not include the location of the Consolan station.

When the Mercator chart shows the location of the Consolan transmitter, provided the difference in longitude between the transmitter and the ship does not exceed 5°, it is necessary only to convert the true bearing, as taken from the tables, to a Mercator bearing, as described in the section on converting great-circle direction to Mercator direction. The Mercator bearing thus derived is then plotted on the chart as an LOP.

When the Mercator chart does not show the area in which the transmitting station is located, the first thing to do is to determine, by mid-latitude sailing, the Mercator bearing of the ship's estimated position, EP, from the transmitting station, as well as the distance. The Consolan tables give the coordinates of the station's position, and by applying to them the coordinates of the EP, the difference of latitude, l, and the difference of longitude, DLo, are found. The direction and distance of the EP from the station can then be determined.

The next step is to convert the great-circle bearing received from the Consolan station to a Mercator bearing. This can be done by means of the conversion table included with the Consolan tables, but, if the difference of longitude between the ship and station does not exceed 5°, it can be done by the formula

tan conversion angle = sin mid-latitude × tan 0.5 difference of longitude

In applying this conversion angle to the true bearing received from the station, it must be borne in mind that the great-circle bearing always lies more towards the elevated pole than does the Mercator bearing.

The Mercator bearing thus found is compared with the Mercator bearing calculated by mid-latitude sailing, and the difference is noted; also noted is the direction of the received bearing relative to the calculated bearing. The next factor to be determined is the most probable position, MPP, and this lies at the end of a perpendicular dropped from the EP to the Mercator bearing received from the station. The length of this perpendicular is found by the law of sines. The distance of the EP from the transmitting station has already been calculated; setting sine 90° against this distance on the **D** scale, the length of the perpendicular is found on the **D** scale under the sine of the difference between the received bearing and the calculated Mercator bearing.

The direction in which the perpendicular is drawn from the EP is determined by applying 90° to the direction of the received bearing. Thus, if the calculated bearing is 162.°0, and the received bearing is 163.°2, the perpendicular will lie in the direction 253.°2 from the EP (163.°2 + 90° = 253.°2).

If a plot of the Consolan LOP is desired, it is drawn through the MPP in accordance with the received bearing, converted to a Mercator bearing.

Example: Our EP is L 41° 17.′0 N, λ 71° 33.′0 W, when we receive a Consolan count of 58 dots (270.°7 True) from the Nantucket station, whose call letters are TUK. We have the Consolan tables, but neither a Consolan nor any other chart that includes both the Nantucket Consolan station and our EP. The Consolan tables give the location of TUK as L 41° 15′ 35″ N (L 41° 15.′6 N), λ 70° 09′ 19″ W (λ 70° 09.′3 W). We wish to plot the Consolan LOP on our chart.

We first determine our Mercator bearing and distance from TUK by mid-latitude, Lm, sailing formulae

TUK	L 41° 15.′6 N	λ 70° 09.′3 W
EP	L 41° 17.′0 N	λ 71° 33.′0 W
l	1.′4 N	*DLo* 1° 23.′7 W = 83.′7 W
Lm	41° 16.′3 N	

The *DLo* of 83.'7 gives a departure, *p*, of 63.0 miles, and our Mercator bearing from TUK is $271°\,16.'5 \left(\dfrac{1.4}{63.0} = \tan 1°\,16.'5 + 270° = 271°\,16.'5\right)$; we will call it 271.°3. In this case, the distance from TUK, computed by slide rule, is the same as *p*, 63.0 miles (sin 1° 16.'5 : 1.4 : : 88° 43.'5 : 63.0).

The next step is to convert the true bearing received from TUK to a Mercator bearing. This can be done either by using the Consolan conversion table, or by calculation. Interpolating for the difference in longitude in the table, the conversion angle is 0.°4. By slide rule, using the conversion formula

$$\text{tan conversion angle} = \sin Lm \times \tan \frac{DLo}{2}$$

we find the tangent to be 0.00802, or 0° 27.'6, which for practical purposes is 0.°5. Since we are West of TUK, the sign will be (−)

Bearing received from TUK	(−)	270.°7 True
Conversion angle		0.°5
Mercator bearing from TUK by signal		270.°2

We now compare the Mercator bearing we got by using our EP with the Mercator bearing we obtained by signal

Calculated Mercator bearing from TUK	271.°3
Mercator bearing from TUK by signal	270.°2
Difference	1.°1

The Consolan LOP, then, lies to the southward of our EP; the next step is to determine our MPP, which will lie at the end of a perpendicular dropped from the EP to the Consolan LOP. Since the distance between the EP and TUK has been established at 63.0 miles, the length of this perpendicular can be determined by the law of sines to be 1.2 miles (90° : 63 : : 1° 06' : 1.21). We can now plot the MPP on the chart, and draw the TUK Consolan LOP through it, in the direction 090.°2 − 270.°2.

Note: Since the above was written, the Consolan station at Nantucket, TUK, has been closed. However, the principles given are applicable to any Consolan or Consol station in the world. As of this printing, the San Francisco station, SFI, is the only active one in the United States.

Plane Sailing

In plane sailing the figure formed by the meridian passing through the point of departure, the parallel of latitude passing through the destination, and the course line, is considered to be a plane right-angled triangle (*see* Figure 9). As in any right triangle, if a second angle and the length of any side are known, the remaining angle and the length of either other side can readily be found by means of the formulae given below.

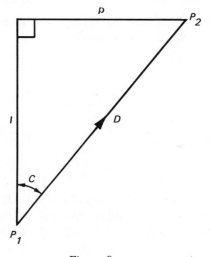

Figure 9

In this triangle, P_1 represents the point of departure and P_2 the destination. The side p, called the "departure," is the distance, in nautical miles, East or West, made good in proceeding to the destination. The side l is the portion of a meridian drawn from the point of departure to the parallel of latitude of the destination; it represents the difference of latitude and is measured in nautical miles, which are equal to minutes of arc along a meridian. The side D represents the distance sailed in nautical miles; the angle C represents the course angle.

Note: In plane sailing, the course is reckoned as course angle from North or South to 90° East or West. Thus, Cn 162° would be written as S 18° E, and Cn 341° as N 19° W.

Plane-sailing formulae are

Given C and D, to find l

$$l = \cos C \times D \tag{1}$$

Given C and D, to find p

$$p = \sin C \times D \tag{2}$$

Given l and p, to find C

$$\tan C = \frac{p}{l} \tag{3}$$

Here, it must be remembered that if l is greater than p, C will be less than 45°; if it is less, C will be greater than 45°.

Given C and l, to find D

$$D = \frac{l}{\cos C} \tag{4}$$

Given C and p, to find D

$$D = \frac{p}{\sin C} \tag{5}$$

Knowing p, it is often necessary to convert it to difference of longitude, DLo. Strictly speaking, this problem does not belong under the heading of plane sailing; it is included here as a matter of convenience. The formula is

$$DLo = \frac{p}{\cos L} \tag{6}$$

where L represents latitude.

Alternatively, if DLo is known, p may be found

$$p = DLo \times \cos L \tag{7}$$

Examples illustrating the use of these formulae are given below.

Example 1: We have steamed 90 miles on Cn 320° and need to find the difference of latitude, *l*. The first step is to convert 320° to N 40° W. Formula (1) then becomes

$$l = \cos 40° \times 90 = 69$$

The difference of latitude, therefore, is 69.′0, or 1°09.′0 North.

Example 2: Given the same data as in Example 1, to find *p* Formula (2) becomes

$$p = \sin 40° \times 90 = 57.9$$

The departure, therefore, is 57.9 miles West.

Example 3a: Given an *l* of 69.′0 South and a *p* of 57.9 miles West, we wish to find *C*. Formula (3) becomes

$$\tan C = \frac{57.9}{69} = 0.839$$

The course angle, therefore, is S 40° W, or Cn 220°.

Example 3b: Given an *l* of 57.9 North and a *p* of 69 miles East, to find *C*, Formula (3) becomes

$$\tan C = \frac{69}{57.9} = 1.19$$

C is greater than 1.0 and the course angle is, therefore, N 50° E, or Cn 050°.
In this example, the **CI** scale was not used; 50°, usually marked in red, was directly above the right-hand index of the **D** scale, which corresponds to 1.19 on the **CI** scale.

Example 4: Given Cn 273.°5, or N 86.°5 W and an *l* of 5 miles, to find *D*, Formula (4) becomes

$$D = \frac{5}{\cos 86° \, 30'} = 81.9$$

The distance, therefore, is 81.9 miles. Cos 86° 30′ is found on the **ST** scale, where it is read as 3° 30′ (90° − 86° 30′).

Example 5: Given Cn 030°, or N 30° E and *p* 41.5 miles, to find *D*, Formula (5) becomes

$$D = \frac{41.5}{\sin 30°} = 83.0$$

The distance, therefore, is 83.0 miles.

Example 6: Given L 46° N and *p* 57.9 miles West, to find the *DLo*, Formula (6) becomes

$$DLo = \frac{57.9}{\cos 46°} = 83.4$$

The difference of longitude, therefore, is 83.'4 West.

Example 7: Given L 43° N and DLo 41.'0 W, to find *p*, Formula 7 becomes

$$p = \cos 43° \times 41 = 30.0$$

The departure, therefore, is 30.0 miles West.

Offshore Navigation

Mid-Latitude Sailing

Mid-latitude sailing is based on approximations which simplify solutions and yield results sufficiently accurate for ordinary navigation over medium distances, say, to 1,200 miles. When the distance is greater, or in high latitudes, or when a rigorous solution is required, great-circle sailing should be used.

When course and distance steamed are given, mid-latitude sailing permits determination of the difference of latitude, l, and the departure, p, expressed as a difference of longitude, DLo, in minutes of arc. Alternatively, when the coordinates of two points are given, it permits determination of the rhumb-line course and the distance between them, D.

In mid-latitude sailing, departure and difference of longitude may be interconverted, using the mean, or mid, latitude, Lm. The formulae are

$$p = DLo, \text{ in minutes} \times \cos Lm \qquad (1)$$

$$DLo, \text{ in minutes} = \frac{p}{\cos Lm} \qquad (2)$$

$$\tan C = \frac{p}{l} \qquad (3)$$

where l is in minutes of arc and C is the course angle, expressed from North or South towards East or West to 90°.

$$D = \frac{l}{\cos C} \qquad (4)$$

Example 1: By mid-latitude sailing, what is the course and what is the distance from Brenton Reef Light (off Newport, R.I.), L 41° 26′ N, λ 71° 23′ W, to St. David's Light, Bermuda, L 32° 22′ N, λ 64° 39′ W?

We set up the problem

$$
\begin{array}{ll}
L_1 \\
L_2
\end{array} \sim
\begin{array}{l}
41^\circ\,26'\,\text{N} \\
32^\circ\,22'\,\text{N}
\end{array}
\qquad\qquad
\begin{array}{ll}
\lambda_1 \\
\lambda_2
\end{array} \sim
\begin{array}{l}
71^\circ\,23'\,\text{W} \\
64^\circ\,39'\,\text{W}
\end{array}
$$

$$
l \qquad 9^\circ\,04'\,\text{S} = 544'\,\text{S} \qquad DLo \quad 6^\circ\,44'\,\text{E} = 404'\,\text{E}
$$

$$
\begin{array}{l}
\tfrac{1}{2}l \\
L_1
\end{array} \sim
\begin{array}{l}
4^\circ\,32'\,\text{S} \\
41^\circ\,26'\,\text{N}
\end{array}
$$

$$
Lm \qquad 36^\circ\,54'\,\text{N}
$$

Having obtained *Lm*, we proceed to find *p*, using Formula (1)

$$p = 404 \times \cos 36^\circ\,54' = 323 \text{ miles}$$

Having found *p*, 323, we find the course, using Formula (3)

$$\tan C = \frac{323}{544} = 0.594 = \text{S}\,30^\circ\,42'\,\text{E}$$

The true course, therefore, will be 149.°3 (180° − 30.°7).

The final step is to determine the distance, using Formula (4)

$$D = \frac{544}{\cos 30^\circ\,42'} = 633 \text{ miles}$$

Thus, the course to reach St. David's Light is 149.°3 and the distance is 633 miles. This calculation compares quite well with a rigorous great-circle solution, which makes the distance 632.2 miles and the initial heading 147° 47.'4.

Example 2: We steam 960 miles on course 230° from L 33° 16′ N, λ 29° 43′ W, and need to find the latitude and longitude of our position.

By substituting S 50° W for 230°, and transposing Formula (4), we can find *l*.

$$l = 960 \times \cos 50^\circ = 617\,\text{S}$$

Knowing that *l* equals 617′ S, or 10° 17′ S, and consequently that L_2 is 22° 59′ N (L 33° 16′ N ∼ 10° 17′ S), we can find *p*, by transposing Formula (3)

$$p = \tan C\,50^\circ \times 617 = 1.19 \times 617 = 735 \text{ miles}$$

To find the DLo, we must first determine Lm

$$l = 10^\circ\,17'\,\text{S, and } \tfrac{1}{2}l = 5^\circ\,08.'5\,\text{S}$$

$$
\begin{array}{ll}
L_1 \\
\tfrac{1}{2}l
\end{array} (-)
\begin{array}{l}
33^\circ\,16.'0\,\text{N} \\
5^\circ\,08.'5\,\text{S}
\end{array}
$$

$$
Lm \qquad 28^\circ\,07.'5\,\text{N}
$$

Then, Formula (2) becomes

$$DLo = \frac{735}{\cos Lm\, 28°\, 07.'5} = 834'$$

Converting 834' to degrees and minutes, we get 13° 54' W.

Finally we can obtain the latitude and longitude of our destination as follows:

$$
\begin{array}{llll}
L_1 & 33°\,16'\,\text{N} & \lambda_1 & 29°\,43'\,\text{W} \\
\sim & 10°\,17'\,\text{S} & DLo\ + & 13°\,54'\,\text{W} \\
\hline
L_2 & 22°\,59'\,\text{N} & \lambda_2 & 43°\,37'\,\text{W}
\end{array}
$$

which are the coordinates of our destination.

Great-Circle Sailing

The shortest distance between any two points on the Earth lies along the great circle that passes through them. Great-circle sailing is used when the distance between the points of departure and arrival, measured along a great circle, is materially shorter than along the rhumb line drawn between them. It is impossible for a ship to steam along a great circle on the same course, unless she is moving due North, due South, or along the equator. It is customary, therefore, to select a number of points along the great-circle track, usually 5° of longitude apart, and steam rhumb-line courses between them; the distance thus steamed closely approximates that of the great-circle track.

Alternatively, the great-circle track may be broken up into equal segments of arc, each of which in the following example is 6°, or 360 nautical miles, in length.

A great-circle voyage should not, of course, be undertaken if the great circle crosses land or dangerous waters, or if such a voyage would take the ship into too high a latitude. Another factor that must be taken into account is the location of the vertex, or point of greatest latitude, through which the circle passes. The vertex might lie beyond the destination, behind the point of departure, or between the two.

The slide rule permits easy solution of great-circle problems by means of various spherical trigonometry formulae. When the distance is great, say, over 3,000 miles, solutions may be determined with considerable accuracy. In any event, the lengthy computations involved may be checked rapidly by slide rule.

In order to solve a problem, it is necessary first to establish the distance along the great-circle track to the destination, the initial heading, and the latitude and longitude of the vertex. Even when the vertex lies beyond the destination, its position must be calculated, because it is used in obtaining the coordinates of the intermediate points at which rhumb-line course changes are to be made.

Two formulae for finding the distance, D, are included: the cosine D formula, Formula (1), is best suited for distances over 4,050 miles (45°), while for distances shorter than this, better results will be obtained by use of the sine D formula, Formula (11).

After these data have been obtained, the coordinates of the points along the great circle at which the course is to be changed must be calculated.

The distance, D, expressed as arc, is first determined, and the formula is

$$\cos D = \sin L_1 \, (\pm) \sin L_2 \sim \cos L_1 \times \cos L_2 \times \cos DLo \qquad (1)$$

where L_1 is the latitude of the point of departure, L_2 the latitude of the destination, and DLo is the difference of longitude between the two places. The following rules are used with this formula:

If DLo is less than 90°, and

a) L_1 and L_2 have the same name, the sign is $(+)$
b) L_1 and L_2 have opposite names, the sign is $(\sim)$.

If DLo is greater than 90°, and

a) L_1 and L_2 have the same name, the sign is $(\sim)$
b) L_1 and L_2 have opposite names, the sign is $(+)$.

If the DLo is greater than 90°, use 180° − DLo instead of the DLo. The distance may be greater than 90° (5,400 miles), in which case the angle found by Formula (1) is subtracted from 180° to obtain the distance in angle. Distance in nautical miles is found by multiplying the number of degrees by 60, then adding the number of minutes.

Should there be a question as to whether or not distance, D, is greater than 90°, it may be resolved as follows. First, find the value of the auxiliary angle, R, using the formula

$$\sin R = \sin DLo \times \cos L_2 \qquad (2)$$

Having found R, a second auxiliary angle, K, is found

$$\sin K = \frac{\sin L_2}{\cos R} \qquad (3)$$

K will be greater than 90° if DLo is greater than 90°, in which case use K_1, where $K_1 = 180° - K$.

Then D is greater than 90° if

a) L_1 and L_2 are of the same name, and K or K_1 is greater than $L_1 + 90°$, or
b) L_1 and L_2 are of opposite name, and K or K_1 is greater than $90° - L_1$.

Because K will, at times, have a value falling between 80° and 90°, very careful interpolation is necessary. Even so, the exact value of D, when near 90°, cannot be determined with this formula.

The initial great-circle heading, C, is usually found by the formula

$$L_2 \sin \text{heading} C = \frac{\cos L_2 \times \sin DLo}{\sin D} \qquad (4)$$

where D is the distance, expressed in angle.

The heading thus found will be similar to azimuth angle, and will have to be applied to 000° or 180° in an easterly or westerly direction.

The initial heading may also be found by the tangent formula, which may give better results if the heading is greater than 45°

$$\tan \text{heading} C = \frac{\sin DLo}{\cos L_1 \tan L_2 (\pm) \sin L_1 \cos DLo} \qquad (5)$$

In this formula, when DLo is less than 90° and L_1 and L_2 have the same name, the sign in the divisor is subtractive; if DLo is greater than 90° the sign is additive. When L_1 and L_2 have opposite names and DLo is less than 90°, the sign is additive.

The next step is to determine the latitude of the vertex, Lv, by the formula

$$\cos Lv = \cos L_1 \times \sin C \qquad (6)$$

after which the longitude of the vertex is obtained. This is done by first determining the DLo between the longitude of the point of departure and that of the vertex, DLo_v

$$\sin DLo_v = \frac{\cos C}{\sin L_v} \qquad (7)$$

then, using the DLo_v, the angular distance from the point of departure to the vertex, Dv, is found by the formula

$$\sin Dv = \cos L_1 \times \sin DLo_v \qquad (8)$$

The next step is to find the latitude, L_x, of each point (X_1, X_2, etc.) along the great-circle track where the ship's course is to be changed. The formula is

$$\sin L_x = \sin L_v \times \cos D_{v-x} \tag{9}$$

D_{v-x} being the angular distance to the vertex, less the angular distance along the great circle at which course is to be changed.

Finally, the longitude of each of these change points is obtained by the formula

$$\sin DLo_{v-x} = \frac{\sin D_{v-x}}{\cos L_x} \tag{10}$$

DLo_{v-x} being the difference between the meridian of DLo_v found in Formula (5) and that of each course change point, X_1, X_2, etc.

Example: Dead Reckoning Altitude and Azimuth Table, U.S. Naval Oceanographic Office, H.O. Publication No. 211, gives an excellent example of great-circle sailing. Let us assume that we have solved a great-circle sailing problem by tables, and wish to use the slide rule to check our results. In each instance, the H.O. No. 211 solution is given in parentheses beside the solution arrived at by slide rule.

We are sailing from San Francisco, L 37° 47.′5 N, λ 122° 27.′8 W to Sydney, Australia, L 33° 51.′7 S, λ 151° 12.′7 E, and wish to check the distance along the great circle, the initial heading, the latitude and longitude of the vertex, and the latitude and longitude of the first point where we will make a course change, as calculated by tables. We decided to space these points 6°, or 360 miles, apart on the great circle.

Since DLo is 86° 19.′5 [360° − (λ_1 + λ_2)], Formula (1) above becomes

$$\cos D = \sin L_1\ 37°\ 47.′5 \times \sin L_2\ 33°\ 51.′7\ S \sim \cos L_1\ 37°\ 47.′5$$
$$\times \cos L_2\ 33°\ 51.′7 \times \cos DLo\ 86°\ 19.′5$$

This gives us

$$\cos D = .341 - .042 = .299 = 72°\ 37'$$

The distance to Sydney being greater than 5,400 miles (90°), we subtract 72° 37′ from 180°, and obtain 107°23′ as the angular distance. This converts to 6,443 miles. (H.O. 211, 6,445.5 miles)

The next step is to find the initial great-circle heading, and to do so, we can use either Formula (4) or Formula (5). Using the distance in angle found by Formula (1), we write Formula (4) as

$$\sin C = \frac{\cos L_2\ 33°\ 51.′7 \times \sin DLo\ 86°\ 19.′5}{\sin D\ 72°37'}$$

We now have

$$\sin C = .869 = C\ 60°\ 30'$$

which is S 60° 30′ W, giving a Cn of 240° 30′. (H.O. 211, 240° 17.′5)

In this instance, it would be preferable to use Formula (5) because C is greater than 45°. DLo being less than 90°, and L_1 and L_2 being of opposite name, the sign in the divisor would be additive, and Formula (5) would become

tan C

$$=\frac{\sin DLo\ 86°\ 19.'5}{\cos L_1\ 37°47.'5\ N \times \tan L_2\ 33°51.'7\ S + \sin L_1\ 37°47.'5\ N \times \cos DLo\ 86°19.'5}$$

From this we obtain

$$\tan C = \frac{0.999}{0.530 + 0.0394} = 1.750 = S\ 60°\ 15'\ W$$

or, Cn 240° 15′. (H.O. 211, 240° 17.′5)

Using Formula (6), we next calculate the latitude of the vertex

$$\cos L_v = \cos L_1\ 37°\ 47.'5 \times \sin C\ 60°\ 15'$$

and obtain

$$\cos L_v = .686 = 46°\ 40'\ S.\ (H.O.\ 211,\ 46°\ 39.'5\ S)$$

The latitude of the vertex is named South, that being the direction of our change of latitude; in solving the problem by the tables, we noted that it lay beyond our destination.

To obtain the longitude of the vertex, we first solve for the difference of longitude between San Francisco and the vertex, DLo_v, and then convert this difference to the actual longitude of the vertex. Formula (7) becomes

$$\sin DLo_v = \frac{\cos C\ 60°\ 15'}{\sin L_v\ 46°\ 35'} = 0.683,\ or\ 43°\ 05'$$

In this case, the vertex lies beyond the destination, and the DLo_v is greater than the DLo of our destination. The DLo_v, therefore, is equal to 180° − 43° 05′, or 136° 55′ W, and it is named West, because our destination lies to the West of us.

To obtain the longitude of the vertex, we add the longitude of San Francisco to the DLo_v, and obtain 259° 32.′8 W. The longitude of the vertex, therefore, will be $100° 27.'2$ E $(360° - 259° 32.'8$ W). (H.O. 211, $100° 29.'7$ E)

Having found DLo_v, we go on to find the distance to the vertex, D_v, using Formula (8)

$$\sin D_v = \cos L_1 \; 37° 47.'5 \times \sin DLo_v \; 43° 05'$$

therefore, $D_v = 0.540$, or $32° 40'$; that is $147° 20'$ $(180° - 32° 40')$. (H.O. 211, $147° 25'$)

We next need the latitude of the first point where we will change course, X_1. This we obtain by Formula (9)

$$\sin L_{x_1} = \sin L_v \; 46° 40' \times \cos D_{v-x} \; 38° 40'$$

Here, $\cos D_{v-x}$ is obtained from D_v, which we found to be $147° 20'$; the points X_1, X_2, etc., are to be $6°$ apart, D_{v-x_1} is therefore $141° 20'$ $(147° 20' - 6°)$, which we write $38° 40'$ $(180° - 141° 20')$.

We now have

$$\sin L_{x_1} = 0.568, \text{ or } 34° 36'$$

The latitude of X_1 is, therefore, $34° 36'$ N. (H.O. 211, $34° 39'$ N)

To obtain the longitude of point X_1, we need to find the difference in longitude between the vertex and point X_1, so we write Formula (10)

$$\sin DLo_{v-x_1} = \frac{\sin D_{v-x_1} \; 38° 40'}{\cos L_x \; 34° 36'} = 0.759 = 49° 23'$$

which we convert to $130° 37'$ $(180° - 49° 23')$. The longitude of point X_1, therefore, equals $259° 32.'8$ W (the longitude of the vertex expressed to the westward), minus $130° 37'$ which makes it $128° 55.'8$. (H.O. 211, $128° 48.'3$ W)

We would proceed to check the coordinates of points X_2, X_3, etc. in a similar manner.

Ordinarily, the coefficients of all the required points "X" are plotted on a Mercator projection chart or charts. The heading for each leg can also be readily determined by mid-latitude sailing, or, if the legs are short, by plane sailing. However, the best method of finding the initial rhumb-line course to the first point X_1, is to apply the conversion angle to the initial great-circle heading. In the example we have been working, the mid-latitude between San Francisco and point X_1 is $36° 11.'8$ N, and one-half the difference of longitude is $3° 14.'0$, so the conversion angle formula becomes

$$\text{tan conversion angle} = \sin 36° 11.'8 \times \tan 3° 14.'0 = .0325$$

The conversion angle, therefore, is $1° 52.'0$. We then subtract $1° 52.'0$ from the initial great-circle heading, $240° 15'$, and have the initial Mercator course, $238.°4$, to the nearest tenth of a degree.

When the distance to be determined is less than 1,800 miles (30°) or greater than 9,000 miles ($180° - 30°$), the accuracy of the solution may often be increased by first solving for the initial heading, using Formula (5) above

$$\tan \text{ heading } C = \frac{\sin DLo}{\cos L_1 \tan L_2 \, (\pm) \sin L_1 \cos DLo}$$

When DLo is less than 90°, the sign in the divisor is ($+$) when L_1 and L_2 are of opposite name, and ($\sim$) when they are of the same name. When DLo is greater than 90°, the sign is ($\sim$) if L_1 and L_2 are of opposite name, and ($+$) if they are of the same name.

Having found the initial heading, the distance may be calculated, using the formula

$$\sin D = \frac{\cos L_1 \sin L_2 \, (\pm) \sin L_1 \cos L_2 \cos DLo}{\cos C} \qquad (11)$$

where, with DLo less than 90°, the sign in the dividend is ($+$) when L_1 and L_2 are of opposite name, and ($\sim$) when they are of the same name. With DLo greater than 90°, the reverse is true, and the sign is ($\sim$) if L_1 and L_2 are of opposite name, and ($+$) if they are of the same name.

Example: We require the initial heading and distance from Cape Race, Newfoundland, $L 46° 39'$ N, $\lambda 53° 05'$ W, to Fastnet Rock, off the south coast of Ireland, $L 51° 23'$ N, $\lambda 9° 36'$ W.

The first step is to obtain the DLo, which is $43° 29'$ ($53° 05' - 9° 36'$). We can now proceed to find the initial heading, C, writing Formula (5)

$$\tan C = \frac{\sin 43° 29'}{\cos 46° 39' \times \tan 51° 23' \, (\sim) \sin 46° 39' \times \cos 43° 29'}$$

Note that the sign in the divisor is ($\sim$), because DLo is less than 90° and L_1 and L_2 are of the same name. Then

$$\tan C = \frac{0.688}{0.860 - 0.528} = \frac{0.688}{0.332} = 2.072 = 64° 15'$$

Since Fastnet lies to the East and North of Cape Race, the initial heading, Cn, is 064° 15′. We can now proceed to find the distance, using Formula (11)

$$\sin D = \frac{\cos 46°\,39' \times \sin 51°\,23'\,(\sim)\,\sin 46°\,39' \times \cos 51°\,23' \times \cos 43°\,29'}{\cos 64°\,15'}$$

where D represents the distance, and the sign in the divisor is ($\sim$) because L_1 and L_2 are both N, and DLo is less than 90°. We can now write

$$\sin D = \frac{0.536 \sim 0.329}{\cos 64°\,15'}$$
$$= \frac{0.207}{\cos 64°\,15'}$$
$$= 0.4765$$
$$= 28°\,28'$$

The distance, therefore, is 1,708 miles (28° × 60 + 28′).

Sextant Altitude Correction

Dip of the Horizon

The dip of the horizon, caused by the fact that the Earth is a sphere, is the angle by which the visible horizon differs from the true horizontal at the observer's eye. Its value increases as the height of the observer's eye increases; it is also affected by terrestrial refraction, the bending of the light rays as we look at the horizon, which increases the distance to the horizon. Furthermore, it can be very considerably affected by anomalous atmospheric conditions, such as a difference between the temperature of the water surface and that of the air above it.

The following formula for determining dip allows for terrestrial refraction in "normal" atmospheric conditions

$$D = 0.97 \sqrt{h}$$

D being the dip in minutes of arc, and h being the observer's height of eye above sea level, in feet.

The value of the dip is subtracted from the sextant altitude for all celestial observations.

Example: Your height of eye is 63 feet. What is the dip correction? The above formula becomes

$$D = 0.97 \sqrt{63} = 7.7$$

The dip, therefore, is $(-)$ 7.′7.

Dip Short of the Horizon

A celestial observation may be necessary when land or some other obstruction located directly below the body makes the sea horizon invisible. In such a case, provided the distance to the obstruction is known, the waterline of the obstruction may be used as the horizontal reference.

Under such conditions, the dip short of the horizon may be closely approximated by use of the formula

$$D_s = 0.416\, d + 0.566\, \frac{h}{d}$$

where D_s is the dip short of the sea horizon, in minutes of arc; d is the distance to the waterline of the obstruction, expressed in nautical miles; and h is the observer's height of eye above sea level, in feet.

This formula is a simplified version of the one given in *Bowditch*; in the great majority of cases it gives the value of the dip correct to the nearest tenth of a minute. Only when the height of eye is great, and the range to the obstruction is very short does some error arise; for example, if the height of eye were 100 feet, and the range 0.1 miles, the above formula would give a dip of 566.′0, whereas the correct dip would be 565.′8.

The value of the dip is subtracted from the sextant altitude for all celestial observations.

Example: The height of eye is 24 feet, and the distance to the obstruction is 0.75 nautical miles. We require the value of the dip short of the horizon. The formula becomes

$$D_s = (0.416 \times 0.75) + 0.566\, \frac{24}{0.75} = 0.312 + (0.566 \times 32)$$
$$= 0.312 + 18.11 = 18.425$$

The dip, as here calculated, is, therefore, $(-)\,18.′4$, which is correct to the nearest tenth of a minute.

Mean Refraction

Mean refraction is based on a temperature of 50°F. (+10° C) and a barometric pressure of 29.83 inches (1010 millibars), conditions which are considered standard. Corrections for "non-standard" temperature and for "non-standard" barometric pressure are given in the following sections.

It is particularly important to correct mean refraction when observations are to be made at very low altitudes, and it should always be done when the utmost accuracy is desired.

It is good practice to apply the index and dip corrections to the sextant altitude before determining the refraction, especially at low altitudes. The sextant altitude so corrected is termed the apparent altitude, *ha*.

A very close approximation of the mean refraction, Rm, may be obtained by use of the slide rule. None of the following formulae will yield values that are in error by more than 0.′2; in the majority of cases, the error will be less than that. Rm should be read to the nearest tenth of a minute; it is always subtractive. Formulae (1) and (2), below, give identical results.

When using a slide rule, it is simpler to avoid, if possible, tangents of angles over 45° and cotangents of angles under 45°. For altitudes between 45° and 90°, remember that the cotangent of the sextant altitude, corrected for index error and dip, equals the tangent of zenith distance $(90° - ha)$, and use the formula

$$Rm = 0.97 \times \cot ha \tag{1}$$

For altitudes between 15° and 40°, the formula is

$$Rm = \frac{0.97}{\tan ha} \tag{2}$$

and for altitudes between 7° and 15°, the formula is

$$Rm = \frac{0.93}{\tan ha} \tag{3}$$

Rm cannot be readily obtained by slide rule for altitudes below 7°. For such altitudes, see the table given below.

Example 1: After applying the index and dip corrections, the altitude of a star is 48° 53.′7. We require Rm.

Formula (1) becomes

$$Rm = 0.97 \times \cot ha\, 48° 53.′7 = 0.′846$$

Rm, therefore, is $(-)$ 0.′8.

Example 2: After applying the index and dip corrections, the altitude of a celestial body is 36° 02.′7. What is its Rm?

Formula (2) becomes

$$Rm = \frac{0.97}{\tan ha\, 36° 02.′7} = 1.′333$$

Rm, therefore, is $(-)$ 1.'3.

Example 3: After applying the index and dip corrections, the altitude of a body is 7° 14.'2. What is its Rm?

Formula (3) becomes

$$Rm = \frac{0.93}{\tan ha \ 7° \ 14.'2} = 7.'3$$

Rm, therefore, is $(-)$ 7.'3.

Mean Refraction for Altitudes Below 8°

Ha	Rm	Ha	Rm	Ha	Rm	Ha	Rm
° ′	′	° ′	′	° ′	′	° ′	′
0 00	− 34.5	1 12	− 22.9	3 00	− 14.4	5 00	− 9.9
03	33.8	15	22.5	05	14.1	05	9.7
06	33.2	18	22.2	10	13.9	10	9.6
09	32.6	21	21.9	15	13.7	15	9.5
12	32.0	24	21.6	20	13.4	20	9.4
15	31.4	27	21.2	25	13.2	25	9.2
0 18	− 30.8	1 30	− 20.9	3 30	− 13.0	5 30	− 9.1
21	30.3	35	20.5	35	12.7	35	9.0
24	29.8	40	20.0	40	12.5	40	8.9
27	29.2	45	19.5	45	12.3	45	8.8
30	28.7	50	19.1	50	12.1	50	8.7
33	28.2	1 55	18.7	3 55	11.9	5 55	8.6
0 36	− 27.8	2 00	− 18.3	4 00	− 11.8	6 00	− 8.5
39	27.3	05	17.9	05	11.6	10	8.3
42	26.8	10	17.5	10	11.4	20	8.1
45	26.4	15	17.2	15	11.2	30	7.9
48	25.9	20	16.8	20	11.1	40	7.7
51	25.5	25	16.5	25	10.9	6 50	7.6
0 54	− 25.1	2 30	− 16.1	4 30	− 10.7	7 00	− 7.4
0 57	24.7	35	15.8	35	10.6	10	7.2
1 00	24.3	40	15.5	40	10.4	20	7.1
03	24.0	45	15.2	45	10.3	30	7.0
06	23.6	50	14.9	50	10.1	40	6.8
09	23.2	2 55	14.7	4 55	10.0	7 50	6.7
1 12	− 22.9	3 00	− 14.4	5 00	− 9.9	8 00	− 6.6

Refraction for Non-Standard Temperature

To correct refraction when the air temperature differs materially from 50° F., the first step is to determine the mean refraction, Rm, as described in the preceding section. The next step is to find the correction factor, C, and this is done by applying the current temperature to 460, the sign being (+) if the temperature is above 0°, and (−) if it is below 0°. The formula is

$$C = \frac{500 \text{ or } 520}{460 \, (\pm) \, T} \tag{1}$$

in which T is the current temperature in degrees Fahrenheit. For temperatures above 60° F., use 500 in the dividend; when the temperature is below 40° F., use 520. Do not correct for temperatures between 40° and 60°.

Refraction, corrected for non-standard temperature, Rt, is then found by means of the formula

$$Rt = Rm \times C \tag{2}$$

Example 1: The mean refraction is (−) 7.′4, the current temperature is 100° F. We require the mean refraction corrected for temperature.

Our first step is to find the value of the correction factor, C, and Formula (1) becomes

$$C = \frac{500}{460 \, (+) \, 100} = \frac{500}{560} = 0.89$$

Formula (2) then becomes

$$Rt = (-)7.′4 \times 0.89 = (-)6.′59$$

The refraction, corrected for temperature, is therefore (−) 6.′6.

Example 2: The mean refraction is (−) 7.′4, the current temperature is (−) 20°. We require the mean refraction corrected for temperature. Here, Formula (1) becomes

$$C = \frac{520}{460 \, (-) \, 20} = \frac{520}{440} = 1.182$$

and Formula (2) becomes

$$Rt = (-)7.′4 \times 1.182 = (-)8.′7$$

The refraction, corrected for temperature, is therefore (−) 8.′7.

Refraction for Non-Standard Barometric Pressure

Non-standard barometric pressure affects the mean refraction less than does non-standard temperature, and ordinarily no allowance need be made for it. However, when the existing pressure varies considerably from the standard, 29.83 inches, it may be desirable to correct for it, particularly at low altitudes.

The mean refraction, corrected for barometric pressure, Rp, at the standard temperature of 50° F., may be found by the formula

$$Rp = Rm \times \frac{EP}{29.83}$$

where Rm is the mean refraction and EP is the existing barometric pressure in inches.

Example: The mean refraction is $(-)7.'4$, the temperature is 50° F., and the barometric pressure is 30.60 inches. We require the refraction corrected for barometric pressure.

The formula becomes

$$Rp = (-)7.'4 \times \frac{30.60}{29.83} = (-)7.'6$$

The refraction corrected for barometric pressure is, therefore, $(-)7.'6$.

Refraction for Combined Non-Standard Temperature and Non-Standard Barometric Pressure

When the mean refraction, Rm, is to be corrected for non-standard conditions of both temperature and barometric pressure, the difference between Rm and the correction for non-standard barometric pressure, Rp, is applied to the correction for non-standard temperature, Rt.

Example: Mean refraction is $(-)7.'4$, the barometric pressure is 30.60 inches, and the temperature is $(-)20°$ F.

The pressure being 30.60 inches, Rp is $(-)7.'6$, and the difference between Rm, $(-)7.'4$, and Rp, is therefore $(-)0.'2$.

The Rm, $(-)7.'4$, corrected for temperature, determined in the same way as is refraction for non-standard temperature, is $(-)8.'7$. To this the Rp correction, $(-)0.'2$, is applied, to give a total of $(-)8.'9$, which is the refraction corrected for both temperature and pressure.

73

Sun's Semidiameter and Parallax

When the Sun and the Moon are observed with a marine sextant, either the lower or the upper limb is brought to the visible horizon. A correction must therefore be made to refer the body's center to the horizon.

This correction for the Moon is included in the consolidated Moon correction tables at the back of the *Nautical Almanac*. It will not be discussed in this text, as it is impractical to include here long-term ephemeristic data for the Moon.

The values for the semidiameter correction for the Sun for every day of the year will be found in Table F of the *Long-Term Sun Almanac* included herein. The correction, as taken from Table F, is to be added to the sextant altitude when the lower limb is observed, and subtracted when the upper limb is observed.

An additional correction of $(+)0.'1$ for parallax should be applied to all observations of the Sun with altitudes between $0°$ and $65°$.

Sea-Air Temperature Difference

The preceding formula for calculating the dip of the horizon is based, as are the values for dip given in the *Nautical Almanac*, on the fact that as altitude increases, standard or "normal" temperature and pressure in the atmosphere decrease. When there is a difference between the temperature of the sea water and the temperature of the air in contact with it, the normal decrease in air temperature is upset, and the normal value of the dip is affected

Considerable study, with varying results, has been devoted to determining the exact effect of such a temperature difference on the value of the dip, with varying results. However, it has been determined that where the water is warmer than the air, the horizon is depressed, resulting in sextant altitudes which are too great; the converse is true if the water is the cooler.

The Japanese Hydrographic Office, after much empiric testing, found that the value of the dip would be affected by 0.11 minutes of arc for each degree Fahrenheit of difference between sea and air temperatures.

As a formula this is stated:

Sea-Air temperature correction $= 0.'11 \times$ difference in temperature in degrees Fahrenheit between sea and air

The correction is subtractive if the air is colder than the water, and additive if it is warmer.

In practice, the dry bulb temperature is taken in the shade at the observer's height of eye, and the water temperature is taken either from a sample obtained in a dip bucket, or from the intake water temperature obtained from the engine room.

Example: The air temperature is 32°F., and the water temperature is 48° F. We require the sea-air temperature correction.

We write the formula

$$\text{S-A correction} = 0.'11 \times 16 = 1.76$$

The correction to the sextant altitude for the sea-air temperature difference is therefore $(-)1.'8$, the sign being subtractive as the water is warmer than the air.

Sun, Stars, and Planets

1. To all sights, apply:

   a. The instrument correction, if any, obtained from the sextant certificate, which may be $(+)$ or $(-)$.

   b. The index correction, obtained by observation, which may be $(+)$ or $(-)$.

   c. The correction for height of eye, or dip, which is always $(-)$.

   d. The correction for the difference between sea temperature and air temperature, which may be $(+)$ or $(-)$.

The above corrections, applied to the sextant altitude, give the apparent altitude, *ha.*

2. To the apparent altitude of all bodies, apply:

   a. The correction for mean refraction, which is always $(-)$.

   b. If required, the correction for non-standard air temperature, which may be $(+)$ or $(-)$.

   c. The correction for non-standard barometric pressure, which may be $(+)$ or $(-)$.

That completes the corrections for observations of the stars and planets.

For observations of the Sun, in addition to the above, apply:

    a. The correction for semidiameter for the date, found in the *Long-Term Sun Almanac*. This is ($+$) for the lower limb sights, and ($-$) for upper limb sights.

    b. The correction for parallax, ($+$)$0.'1$, for observations at all altitudes below $65°$.

Sight Reduction

To plot the line of position, LOP, resulting from the observation of a celestial body, two computations are required: both the altitude of the body, H, and its azimuth angle, Z, must be calculated. When the modern inspection tables are used, the values of H and Z are obtained together.

However, when reducing observations with the slide rule, two completely separate calculations must be completed to obtain H and Z. Also, to obtain H by means of two of the formulae given in this section, Z must first be computed. It seems desirable, therefore, to consider the determination of Z before going on to H.

In computing azimuths with the slide rule, remember that the quadrant in which the body lies is indeterminate. It is best, therefore, to obtain an approximate azimuth of the body by compass at the time of observation, in order that the proper quadrant may be determined.

In all the formulae for computing azimuth and altitude, L represents latitude, d represents declination, t represents meridian angle, and Ho represents the fully corrected sextant altitude.

Computing Azimuth

Three formulae are available for determining Z with the slide rule. The simplest of these is the sine Z formula

$$\sin Z = \frac{\cos d \sin t}{\cos H} \tag{1}$$

Either Ho or Hc may be used for H in the divisor.

The major limitation on the use of this formula is due to the difficulty in determining the value of Z as it approaches $90°$, a difficulty caused by the compression of the sine scale on the slide rule at its upper end.

Example 1: You are in L 34° N and observe, to the Southwest, a body whose declination, d, is S 22°, meridian angle, t, is 35° W, and corrected sextant altitude, Ho, is 24° 51.′0. Formula (1) becomes

$$\sin Z = \frac{\cos d\, 22° \times \sin t\, 35°}{\cos Ho\, 24°\, 51'} = 0.586$$

The azimuth angle, therefore, is S 35° 50′ W, and azimuth reckoned from the North, Zn, is 215.°8 (180° + 35.°8).

The second formula is the cosine Z formula, which gives very good results for azimuth angles; it is particularly useful when the value of t is not known.

$$\cos Z = \frac{\sin d\, (\pm)\, \sin H\, \sin L}{\cos H\, \cos L} \tag{2}$$

The rule for determining the sign in the dividend is that it is positive when L and d are of opposite name; when L and d are of the same name, it is subtractive, and the smaller quantity is subtracted from the larger.

Example 2: In L 34° N, you observe, to the North and East, a body whose altitude, Ho, is 20° 08.′0, and whose declination is N 19° 43.′7. What is azimuth reckoned from the North, Zn?

Formula (2) becomes

$$\cos Z = \frac{\sin d\, 19°\, 43.'7\, (\pm)\, \sin Ho\, 20°\, 08.'0 \times \sin L\, 34°}{\cos Ho\, 20°\, 08.'0 \times \cos L\, 34°}$$

L and d being of the same name, the sign is subtractive.

Therefore, $\cos Z = \dfrac{0.1446}{0.778}$ or 0.186

and $Z =$ N 79° 17′ E
which gives a Zn of 079.°3.

The third formula is the tangent Z formula. This formula is particularly useful if the altitude is not known, or if the body is located near one of the four cardinal points. It gives excellent results at all altitudes.

$$\tan Z = \frac{\sin t}{\cos L\, \tan d\, (\pm)\, \sin L\, \cos t} \tag{3}$$

Where L and d have the same name, and t is less than 90°, the sign in the divisor is subtractive; if t is greater than 90°, the sign is additive.

Where L and d are of opposite name, the sign is additive, t being less than 90°.

With this azimuth formula, bear in mind that the tangent of 45° is 1.0, and that 10.0 is the tangent for approximately 84° 17′. Thus, the values of the tangent of an angle over 45° must be read off the **CI** scale, and if the angle is larger than 84° 17′, its complement must be read off the **ST** scale.

Example 3: Given L 31° N, *d* N 29°, *t* 30° E, and the body located slightly North of East.

The first item to note is that since L and *d* have the same name and *t* is less than 90°, the sign in the divisor will be subtractive. Thus, Formula (3) becomes

$$\tan Z = \frac{\sin t\, 30°}{\cos L\, 31° \tan d\, 29° \sim \sin L\, 31° \cos t\, 30°}$$

After multiplying the two factors in the divisor, we obtain

$$\tan Z = \frac{0.5}{.475 - .446} \text{ or } \frac{0.5}{0.029}$$

This division yields an answer of 17.24 which means that the azimuth will be found on the **ST** scale. With the hairline on the slide set to 1.724 on the **CI** scale, we read 3° 19.′5 on the **ST**; subtracting this from 90°, we find the azimuth angle to be N 86° 40.′5 E, which makes Zn 086.°7.

Computing Altitude

Three formulae can conveniently be used for determining the altitude, H, with the slide rule.

The first is the sine *H* formula, the classic formula for computing H

$$\sin H = \sin L \sin d\, (\pm)\, \cos L \cos d \cos t \qquad (1)$$

where *L* represents latitude, *d* represents declination, and *t* represents meridian angle.

This is the formula that was used for calculating the great majority of the altitudes in the U.S. Naval Oceanographic Office new inspection tables, H.O. Publication No. 229. It was also used for slide-rule reduction of altitudes by a number of naval patrol-bomber navigators during World War II. With a 10-inch rule, altitudes accurate to within about two minutes may be found for altitudes less than 30°. With a 20-inch rule, this same accuracy may be obtained for altitudes up to 50°.

The rules for using the above formula are simple:

If *t* is less than 90° and L and *d* have the same name, the sign is (+); if L and *d* have opposite names, the sign is (∼).

If t is greater than 90° and L and d have the same name, the sign is $(\sim)$; if L and d have opposite names, the sign is $(+)$.

To determine the computed altitude, Hc, it is necessary only to multiply the sine values, and then the cosine values. It is convenient to have a pencil available, so that the two products can be jotted down at one end of the slide. After adding them, or subtracting the smaller from the larger, in accordance with the rule, the writing may be readily erased from the slide rule.

When t is greater than 90°, use $180° - t$, or t_1. Bear in mind that when you go "off the scale," as when using the cosine of 85°, the first digit of the product will be .0.

Example 1: L 14° N, d N 29°, t 94° E. Since t is greater than 90°, we will use t_1, which is 86°; this will be located at the 4° mark on the **ST** scale.

We then obtain for $\sin L \times \sin d$ 0.1173
and for $\cos L \times \cos d \times \cos t_1$ $(-)$ .0592
                                     0.0581

The sign is subtractive, because t is greater than 90°, and L and d have the same name. Over 581 on the **D** scale, read 3° 20.′0 on **ST**.
Hc, therefore, is 3° 20.′0.

The second formula for calculating H is the cosine H formula. This formula yields an accurate value for H at altitudes above 60° when a 10-inch slide rule is used, and above 40° with a 20-inch rule. However, when this formula is employed, Z must be computed by means of the tangent Z formula – Formula (3) in the foregoing section – before H can be computed.

$$\cos H = \frac{\cos L \sin d \, (\pm) \sin L \cos d \cos t}{\cos Z} \tag{2}$$

The sign in the dividend is additive if L and d are of opposite name. If L and d are of the same name and t is less than 90°, it is subtractive, but if t is greater than 90°, it is additive.

Example 2: Our DR latitude was 23° 57.′5 N when we observed the morning Sun to have a corrected altitude of 56° 30.′5, and bearing about 160° True by compass. At the time, the Sun's declination was S 8° 15.′1, t was 9° 29.′3 E. We require the computed Z and H as well as Zn.

We first compute the value of Z, using the tan Z formula, and find the tangent of Z to be 0.309, which makes Z to be S 17° 10′ E, which we will use in computing H, and makes Zn 162.°8.

Using Formula (2) above, we obtain

$$\cos H = \frac{.1312 + .396}{.954} = \frac{.5272}{.954} = .552$$

Note that the sign in the dividend is additive, L and d being of opposite name.

Ha is, therefore, 56° 30.'0.

Applying Ho 56° 30.'5 to this, we obtain an intercept of Towards 0.'5, which we can plot, using Zn 162.°8.

The third formula for computing H is the tangent H formula

$$\tan H = \frac{\dfrac{\sin M}{\tan t} (\pm) \sin d \cos M}{\cos d} \tag{3}$$

Here, the sign in the dividend is additive when L and d are of the same name, and t is less than 90°. If t is greater than 90°, the sign is subtractive. When L and d are of opposite name, the sign is subtractive.

It will be noted that a new factor, M, has appeared on the scene. M is the angle at the geographic position of the body in the navigational triangle, PZM. It is called the parallactic angle.

To find the value of M, we must first compute the value of Z, preferably using the tangent Z formula – Formula (3) in the foregoing section. Having found the value of Z, we can compute M, using the formula

$$\tan M = \frac{\sin Z}{\cos Ho \tan L (\pm) \sin Ho \cos Z} \tag{4}$$

in which the sign in the divisor is additive when L and d are of the same name, and t is less than 90°; when t is greater than 90°, the sign is subtractive, as it also is when L and d are of opposite name.

The altitude may now be computed by means of the tangent H formula – Formula (3) above.

In the following example, we will follow through a complete reduction, first solving for Z, then for M, and finally for H.

Example 3: Our DR is L 30° 03.'4 N, λ 59° 12.'2 W when we observe the morning Sun to have an Ho of 63° 45.'7; its declination at the time of observation was N 17° 02.'6, and its approximate azimuth by compass was 115°. We decide to reduce the observation from an assumed position; our assumed latitude will be 30° N, and by assuming a longitude and applying it to the Sun's Greenwich hour angle, GHA, we find t to be 25° E.

The tangent Z formula becomes

$$\tan Z = \frac{\sin t\, 25°}{\cos L\, 30° \tan d\, 17°\, 02.'6 \sim \sin L\, 30° \cos t\, 25°}$$

$$= \frac{\sin 25°}{0.2655 \sim 0.4533} = \frac{\sin 25°}{0.1878} = 2.250$$

which makes $Z\, 66°\, 04.'0$, or S $66°\, 04.'0$ E; for plotting purposes, it will be $Zn\, 113.°9$.

We now compute the value of M, writing Formula (2)

$$\tan M = \frac{\sin Z\, 66°\, 04.'0}{\cos Ho\, 63°\, 45.'7 \tan L\, 30° + \sin Ho\, 63°\, 45.'7 \cos Z\, 66°\, 04.'0}$$

$$= \frac{\sin Z\, 66°\, 04.'0}{0.2554 + 0.3640} = \frac{\sin Z\, 66°\, 04.'0}{0.6194} = 1.4775$$

M, therefore, is $55°\, 55.'0$.

We can now compute the altitude, and write Formula (3)

$$\tan H = \frac{\dfrac{\sin M\, 55°\, 55.'0}{\tan t\, 25°} + \sin d\, 17°\, 02.'6 \cos M\, 55°\, 55.'0}{\cos d\, 17°\, 02.'6}$$

$$= \frac{1.775 + 0.1645}{\cos d\, 17°\, 02.'6} = \frac{1.9395}{\cos d\, 17°\, 02.'6} = 2.030$$

Hc is therefore $63°\, 46.'0$, and having both the computed altitude and azimuth, we can proceed to plot the observation.

Note: As for the other examples, a 20-inch slide rule with a magnifying glass on the cursor was used for this reduction.

The actual values of Z, M, and Hc compared with those obtained by slide rule are:

	Actual	Slide Rule
Z	$66°\, 03.'25$	$66°\, 04.'0$
M	$55°\, 52.'7$	$55°\, 55.'0$
Hc	$63°\, 45.'7$	$63°\, 46.'0$

Horizon Sights

A horizon sight is an observation of a celestial body obtained when the body is in contact with the sea horizon. The Sun is the body usually used for such observations, for which no sextant is required. The sine H formula, which has already been discussed in connection with computing altitude, lends itself well to the reduction of horizon sights by slide rule. All that is needed is to obtain Greenwich mean time at the moment the Sun's limb is in contact with the horizon and to correct most carefully for dip, refraction, and semidiameter, the resulting altitude of $0°$.

It must be borne in mind that the resulting corrected altitude, Ho, will be negative in value and that, unless the DR position is greatly in error, the computed altitude, Hc, also will be negative. For negative altitudes, if Ho is greater than Hc, the intercept will be *away*, and will be plotted in the direction of the supplement of the azimuths.

Usually, the best way to find the azimuth is to convert it from an amplitude. Alternatively, it may be calculated by means of one of the azimuth formulae discussed in this text.

Low-altitude sights have been considered unreliable, mainly because of the presumed vagaries of refraction at altitudes below $5°$. However, the refraction tables available today almost invariably give good results. In a number of horizon observations of the Sun, the average error was found to be 1.95 miles. This average would undoubtedly have been smaller, had the altitudes been computed to the nearest tenth of a minute, rather than to the nearest minute.

From positions at sea that could be accurately established, the writer made 378 observations of the Sun at altitudes ranging downwards from $5°$ to the horizon. Of these sights, 336 yielded a line-of-position plotting within one mile of the actual position, 38 fell between 1.1 and 2.0 miles of the position, and the remaining 4 fell between 2.0 and 2.2 miles of the position.

Horizon sights can be expected to yield good results in the great majority of cases, and they will yield useful information on position, in the event that no sextant is available. On a clear day in the tropics, it is easy to determine the instant the Sun's upper limb touches the horizon by observing a quite bright greenish-blue flash, known as the "green flash." This flash is caused by the greater refraction of the blue-violet end of the light spectrum, and consequently it remains visible slightly longer than does the red-yellow light.

Example: At sunset, when our DR position was L 35°02.′1 N, λ 69°14.′7 W, we observed the Sun's upper limb to have an altitude of 0°. Greenwich hour angle and declination were 168°05.′7 and N 13°58.′1, respectively, and the semidiameter was 15.′8.

The observer's height of eye was 12 feet, the barometric pressure was 30.27 inches, the sea temperature was 82° F., and the air temperature was 71° F.

We wish to find the computed altitude, Hc, using the sine-cosine formula, and to plot a line of position.

We first correct the altitude, in this instance using the tables in the *Nautical Almanac* and the sea-air temperature formula

$$h_s \; \odot \qquad\qquad\qquad\qquad\qquad\qquad\qquad 0°00.′0$$

$$\text{Dip, 12}' \quad (-) \;\; 3.′4$$

$$R \qquad\quad (-)\,34.′5$$

Additional R,
Nautical Almanac, p. A4 $\qquad (+)\,2.′3$

$$SD \odot \quad (-)\,15.′8$$

Sea-Air Temp. Corr. $(-)\;\; 1.′2$

$$\overline{(-)\,54.′9\,(+)\,2.′3}\;\; \text{Net. Corr.}\quad\dfrac{(-)\,52.′6}{(-)\,0°52.′6}$$

$$Ho$$

where $h_s \; \odot$ represents altitude of the Sun's upper limb, R represents refraction, $SD \odot$ represents semidiameter of the Sun, and Ho represents corrected altitude.

We next obtain the meridian angle, t:

$$\text{Greenwich hour angle} \;\; 168°\,05.′7$$

$$\lambda \quad\;\; 69°\,14.′7\,\text{W}$$

$$t \quad \overline{\;98°\,51.′0\,\text{W}}$$

Since latitude and declination, d, are of the same name and t is greater than 90°, we will use its supplement, 81°09.′0 (180° − 98°51.′0), and write the sine-cosine formula

$$\sin Hc = \sin L\,35°\,02.'1 \times \sin d\,13°\,58.'1\,(-)\cos L\,35°\,02.'1$$
$$\times \cos d\,13°\,58.'1 \times \cos t\,81°\,09.'0$$
$$= 0.1385\,(-)\,0.1221 = 0.0164 = 0°\,56.'4$$

The computed altitude, therefore, is $(-)\,0°\,56.'4$.
We now find the Sun's azimuth angle, Z, using the sine formula

$$\sin Z = \frac{\cos d\,13°\,58.'1 \times \sin t\,81°\,09.'0}{\cos Hc\,0°\,56.'4}$$
$$= \frac{0.97 \times 0.988}{1.0} = 73°\,25'$$

The azimuth angle, therefore, is N $73.°4$ W, Zn is $286.°6\,(360° - 73.°4)$, and, since the negative value of Ho is less than the negative value of Hc, the intercept, a, is

$$Ho\,(-)\,0°\,52.'6$$
$$\underline{Hc\,(-)\,0°\,56.'4}$$
$$3.'8\ \text{Towards.}$$

Time Conversion

Time to Arc

Time may readily be converted into arc by a series of steps on the slide rule. The conversion may be facilitated if the following values are kept in mind:

1 hour = 15°	4 minutes = 1° or 60′	4 seconds = 1′
	1 minute = 0.°25 or 15′	1 second = 0.′25

1. Multiply the number of hours by 15, and note the resulting number as degrees.
2. Divide by 4 the number of minutes, and note the resulting whole number as degrees.
3. Multiply by 15 the number of minutes remaining, and note the resulting number as minutes of arc.
4. Multiply by 0.25 the number of seconds, and note the resulting number as minutes of arc.
5. Add together the number of degrees and minutes of arc obtained in the above four steps.

Example: We wish to convert 13 hours, 46 minutes, 58 seconds, to arc.

		D	M
1. 13 hours × 15	=	195	
2. $\frac{46}{4}$ minutes = 11, with 2 left over	=	11	
3. 2 minutes × 15	=		30
4. 58 seconds × 0.25	=		14.5
5.	=	206	44.5

13 hours 46 minutes 58 seconds converted to arc is, therefore, 206° 44.′5.

Arc to Time

Arc may readily be converted into time by a series of steps on the slide rule. The conversion may be facilitated if the following values are kept in mind:

$$15° = 1 \text{ hour} \qquad 15' = 1 \text{ minute} \qquad 1' = 4 \text{ seconds}$$
$$1° \text{ or } 60' = 4 \text{ minutes} \qquad\qquad 0.'25 = 1 \text{ second}$$

1. Divide the number of degrees by 15, and note the resulting whole number as hours.
2. Multiply by 4 the remaining number of degrees and note the result as minutes.
3. If the number of minutes of arc is greater than 15, divide it by 15, and note the whole number in the dividend as minutes of time. If it is less than 15, treat as in Step 4.
4. Multiply by 4 the remaining number of minutes of arc and the decimal of a minute, and note the answer to the nearest second.
5. Add together the number of hours, minutes, and seconds found in the above four steps.

Example: We wish to convert 329° 59.'6 to time.

<table>
<tr><td></td><td></td><td>H</td><td>M</td><td>S</td></tr>
<tr><td>1.</td><td>$\dfrac{329°}{15} = 21 \text{ hours} + 14° = 21$</td><td>21</td><td></td><td></td></tr>
<tr><td>2.</td><td>$14° \times 4 =$</td><td></td><td>56</td><td></td></tr>
<tr><td>3.</td><td>$\dfrac{59.'6}{15} = 3 \text{ minutes} + 14.'6 =$</td><td></td><td>3</td><td></td></tr>
<tr><td>4.</td><td>$14.'6 \times 4 = 58.4 \text{ seconds} =$</td><td></td><td></td><td>58</td></tr>
<tr><td>5.</td><td>$=$</td><td>21</td><td>59</td><td>58</td></tr>
</table>

329° 59.'6 converted to time is, therefore, 21 hours 59 minutes 58 seconds.

Local Mean Time to Zone Time

The times of some celestial phenomena are first determined as local mean time, LMT, that is, time based on the mean or average Sun, and applying to one particular meridian. However, our clocks aboard ship are almost never set to LMT; they are usually set to zone time, ZT. Zone time is the local mean time of a zone or reference meridian, and is kept throughout a designated zone. Our clocks, therefore, read LMT only when we are exactly on the reference meridian of our zone. If the LMT of sunrise, for example, is to be useful, it must be converted to the time kept by our clocks.

In zone time, the nearest meridian exactly divisible by 15° is usually used as the time zone meridian. Thus, within a time zone extending 7.°5 on each side of the zone meridian, the clock time is the same, and the time in adjacent zones will differ from ours by exactly one hour. Our ZT, therefore, can differ from our LMT by as much as one half hour.

To convert LMT to ZT, we must find the difference in longitude between our own meridian, and our time zone meridian. This difference is then converted into time, one degree being equal to 4 minutes of time, and one minute of arc being equal to 4 seconds of time. Thus 3°43′ of longitude would equal 14 minutes 52 seconds (4 × 3 = 12 minutes + 43 × 4 seconds).

If our ship's longitude is West of our zone meridian, our LMT will be earlier than our ZT, and to convert the LMT to ZT, the difference in longitude between our meridian and the zone meridian, converted to time, must be added to our LMT. Conversely, if we are East of our zone meridian, our LMT will be later than our ZT, and the difference in longitude, stated as time, must be subtracted from our LMT.

Example 1: We are in λ 69° 42.′3 W, and our clocks are set to zone (+) 5 time (zone meridian 75° W). The LMT is 17 53 42. We require zone time.

Our longitude	69° 42.′3 W			
Zone meridian	75° 00.′0 W			
Difference in longitude	5° 17.′7 E			
			H	*M*	*S*
5°	=		20	
17.′7	=		1	11
Difference of longitude in time	= (−)		21	11 E
LMT	=	17	53	42
Zone time	=	17	32	31

The sign is subtractive because we are East of our zone meridian.

Example 2: We are in λ 117° 22.′6 E, and our clocks are set to zone (−) 8 time (zone meridian 120° E). The LMT is 05 12 32. We require the zone time.

Our longitude	117° 22.′6 E
Zone meridian	120° 00.′0 E
Difference in longitude	2° 37.′4 W

			H	*M*	*S*
2°	=			8	
37.′4	=			2	30
Difference of longitude in time	= (+)			10	30 W
LMT	=		05	12	32
Zone time	=		05	23	02

The sign is additive because we are West of our zone meridian.

Time of Local Apparent Noon

A vessel under way can quite accurately determine the time of local apparent noon, LAN, by means of a slide rule, provided that the DR longitude is known reasonably closely and that a *Nautical Almanac* or an *Air Almanac* is available. The *Long-Term Sun Almanac,* included in this text, may also be used. However, for this purpose, an *Air Almanac,* which gives ephemeristic data for every 10 minutes of time, rather than for every hour, is slightly more convenient than a *Nautical Almanac,* and both are much more convenient than the *Long-Term Sun Almanac.*

In the forenoon, while the Sun is still well to the East, enter the *Nautical Almanac,* and extract the tabulated Greenwich hour angle, GHA, of the Sun which is *nearest to, but East of*, your DR longitude, together with the Greenwich mean time, GMT, of this entry. Next, from the DR plot on the chart, determine the longitude for this GMT. Having obtained this longitude, find the difference between it and the Sun's GHA, as taken from the *Almanac.* This difference is meridian angle East, tE, and for this purpose it is expressed in minutes of arc.

Next, in order to establish the time of LAN, it is necessary to determine the instant of time when the Sun's hour circle will coincide with the ship's longitude. This is done by combining the rate of change of longitude of the ship with that of the Sun. The former can be determined from the chart, or by working it as a mid-latitude sailing problem. The latter is an almost uniform 15°, or 900 minutes of arc per hour, towards the West.

If the ship is moving towards the East, the hourly rate of change of longitude is added to that of the Sun; if she is sailing towards the West, it is subtracted from that of the Sun. The result of this combination is then divided into tE, expressed in minutes of arc, as shown in the following formula

$$\text{Interval to } LAN = \frac{t\text{E in minutes of arc}}{900' \, (\pm) \text{ ship's change of longitude per hour}}$$

The answer to this equation will be in decimals of an hour, and should be determined to three significant places. If the answer is multiplied by 60, minutes and decimals of minutes are obtained; the decimals of minutes, multiplied by 60, will in turn yield seconds. The answer, which will be mathematically correct to within about 4 seconds, added to the hour of GMT obtained from the *Nautical Almanac* will give the GMT of LAN at the ship. The ship's time zone description may be applied to the GMT to give the ship's time of LAN.

Example: On 23 March, we are steaming on course 064°, speed 20.0 knots, and we desire to observe the Sun at LAN. At 1140, zone + 4 time, we note that our 1200 DR position will be L 43° 15.′5 N, λ 66° 27.′6 W. Our zone description being plus 4, the GMT of our 1200 position will be 1600.

Turning to the *Nautical Almanac* for 23 March, we find that the Sun's GHA at 1600 GMT will be 58° 20.′1. Subtracting this from our DR longitude for that time, we obtain a difference of 8° 07.′5, or 487.′5; this is the Sun's meridian angle East at 1200.

We elect to find our rate of change of longitude per hour by mid-latitude sailing. Using our 1200 DR position, course 064°, and speed 20.0 knots, we find that the mid-latitude at 1230 will be L 43° 19.′9 N, and that the departure is 17.98 miles per hour. This gives us a rate of change of longitude of 24.′7 per hour to the eastward. The formula, therefore, becomes

$$\text{Interval to } LAN = \frac{487.′5}{875.3\,(900′ - 24.′7)} = 0.557 \text{ hours}$$

0.557 hours multiplied by 60 equals 33.4 minutes; 0.4 minutes multiplied by 60 equals 24 seconds. This, added to 1200, gives us the time of LAN.

The ship's time of LAN will, therefore, be 12 33 24 (+4).

Noon Sights

Solution of Noon Sight

The noon sight can be reduced by means of either of the formulae given for computing altitude at altitudes over 45°; if the cos H formula is used, azimuth angle, Z, may be assumed to be 000° or 180°, as the case may be, without computing it. Computed altitude, Hc, $\sim$ corrected sextant altitude, Ho, determines the intercept in the usual manner. If Ho is the greater, the DR latitude will be altered by the amount of the intercept in the direction of the Sun's bearing, either 000° or 180°. Conversely, if Hc is the greater, the alteration in latitude will be in the direction away from the Sun.

However, the latitude at local apparent noon, LAN, may be accurately determined, without calculating an altitude, by one of three formulae which hinge on the relationship between the Sun's declination, d, and the latitude, L.

The first formula, for use when the latitude and declination are of the same name but the latitude is greater than the declination, is

$$L = 90° + d - Ho \tag{1}$$

in which Ho represents the completely corrected sextant altitude.

When the declination and latitude are of opposite name, the formula is

$$L = 90° - (d + Ho) \tag{2}$$

When latitude and declination are of the same name, but the declination is greater than the latitude, the formula is

$$L = d + Ho - 90° \tag{3}$$

Example 1: Our DR latitude is 37° 45.'0 N, and the Sun's declination at LAN is N 21° 36.'4; the Ho was 73° 50.'2. To find our latitude, we write Formula (1) as

$$L = 90° + 21° 36.'4 - 73° 50.'2 = 37° 46.'2$$

Our latitude at LAN, therefore, is 37° 46.'2 N.

Example 2: At LAN we were in DR L 18° 12.'8 S, the declination was N 14° 51.'2, and the Ho was 56° 55.'6. Latitude and declination being of opposite name, we here use Formula (2), which becomes

$$\begin{aligned} L &= 90° - (14° 51.'2 + 56° 55.'6) \\ &= 90° - 71° 46.'8 \\ &= 18° 13.'2 \end{aligned}$$

Our latitude, therefore, was 18° 13.'2 S.

Example 3: Our DR latitude at LAN was 12° 14.'5 N, at which time the Sun's declination was N 21° 29.'7; the Ho was 80° 46.'5. As latitude and declination are of the same name, we select Formula (3), and write

$$L = 21° 29.'7 + 80° 46.'5 - 90° = 12° 16.'2$$

At LAN our latitude, therefore, was 12° 16.'2 N.

Fixes in Conjunction with Noon Sight

Excellent running fixes may be obtained in conjunction with the noon sight when the Sun's declination is within about 30° of the ship's latitude.

If we desire a change of azimuth of about 45° between sights for a running fix obtained before and after noon, the time to make the observations can be approximated. All that is necessary is to find the numerical difference between the latitude and the declination; this will approximate the meridian angle when the sun will be 45° in azimuth angle from the meridian. The meridian angle thus found, multiplied by 4, will give the time in minutes relative to the time of LAN at which the observation is to be made.

Example 1: Our expected latitude at LAN will be 33° 16' N, and the Sun's declination, *d*, at that time will be N 20° 37.'0.

Now 33° 16' − 20° 37' = 12° 39', or 12.°65, and 12.65 × 4 = 50.6

The Sun, therefore, will bear about 135°, 51 minutes before LAN, and about 225°, 51 minutes after LAN.

Example 2: L 10°07′ S, *d* N 11°12′. Here, as L and *d* are of opposite name, we add them to find the numerical difference. 10°07′ + 11°12′ = 21°19′; for our purpose, we will call it 21.°3, and 21.3 × 4 = 85.2 minutes.

The Sun, therefore, will bear 45° from our meridian 85 minutes before and after LAN.

Example 3: L 8°53′ N, *d* N 21°16′. 21°16′ − 8°53′ = 12°23′; call it 12.°4. 12.4 × 4 = 49.6.

The Sun, therefore, will bear about 045° some 50 minutes before LAN, and about 315°, 50 minutes after.

Longitude at Local Apparent Noon

Because of the compression of the sine scale, the classic sine formula – Formula (1) in the section on computing altitude – does not lend itself well for use with a 10-inch slide rule when the altitude is greater than 30°, nor does the cosine *H* formula for altitudes below 60°.

However, if the day is clear, and an almanac and the correct time are available, the ship's longitude at local apparent noon, LAN, can be approximated by what is generally called the "equal morning and afternoon altitude method." This, as we shall see, is a misnomer, because the afternoon altitude, which we will call the PM-H, is equal to the morning altitude, AM-H, only when a vessel is proceeding due East or due West, and the Sun's declination does not change between the AM-H and PM-H. The latitude at LAN can, of course, also be determined, thus yielding a close approximation of the true position at that time.

The best results are obtained when the AM-H is obtained while the Sun is still changing altitude fairly rapidly; that is, when its azimuth is not more than 140° True. In summer, in lower and mid-latitudes, the change in azimuth is very rapid, and the AM-H may be obtained only a short time before LAN. However, when the latitude and declination are, for example, 50° apart, the AM-H may have to be obtained more than 2 hours before LAN.

The technique in the equal altitude method was to obtain an AM-H, noting the sextant angle and the time of observation. After observing the Sun at LAN, the sextant was reset to the AM-H, and the time was taken when the Sun again reached the same altitude. However, for the new equivalent-altitude method, which yields far better results than the old, it is best to graph both the AM and PM altitudes, plotting altitudes against Greenwich mean time, GMT; a line of "best fit" is then drawn through, or as close as possible to, the plotted altitudes. An altitude from the AM graph is selected and its GMT is noted.

As stated above, the PM-H will differ from the AM-H if the ship is changing latitude, or if the Sun is changing in declination between these two observations. Allowance can be made for each of these two factors.

The approximate effect of the ship's change of latitude on the PM-H can be determined by use of a correction factor, the cosine of the azimuth angle, Z, at the time the AM-H was obtained. Since it is usually difficult to obtain good azimuths at sea at altitudes higher than a few degrees, this may be approximated by means of the formula

$$\sin Z = \frac{\cos d \times \sin t}{\cos Ho} \tag{1}$$

in which d is the Sun's declination, t the Sun's meridian angle found by using the best estimate of the longitude at the time of AM-H, and Ho the corrected sextant angle.

Having thus found the value of Z, at LAN we find the difference in latitude since our best estimate of our latitude at the time of AM-H, double it, and multiply it by the cosine of Z. The result, in minutes of arc, is applied to AM-H, the sign being $(+)$ if the change in latitude has brought us nearer the Sun, and $(-)$ if away from the Sun.

The effect of the change in declination may similarly be determined by means of the cosine of M, the angle at the Sun's geographic position in the navigational triangle PZM, in which P is the elevated pole, and Z the ship's position. The angle M is found by the formula

$$\sin M = \frac{\cos L \times \sin t}{\cos Ho} \tag{2}$$

in which t and Ho are determined as in Formula (1), and L is the latitude obtained at LAN.

Having found the value of M, we determine its cosine. Incidentally, in H.O. 214, the factor "Δd," used for correcting the tabulated altitude for minutes of declination over the tabulated declination, is the cosine of M stated to two decimal places.

We estimate the time of LAN, that is, the mid-time of the period during which the maximum altitudes were obtained, and find the difference between this time and the time of AM-H. This difference is doubled, and then multiplied by cosine M; the result in minutes is applied to AM-H, the sign being $(+)$ if the change in declination is bringing the Sun nearer the ship, and $(-)$ if away from the ship.

When both corrections have been applied to AM-H, we have the value of PM-H. For this sight, we commence observing the Sun when it is somewhat higher than the value of PM-H, and again make a string of observations, the final one being when the altitude is below PM-H. These sights are again plotted against time, and a line of "best fit" is drawn in. The altitude of PM-H is next found on this line, and the corresponding GMT is noted.

We now proceed to determine the GMT of LAN, that is, when the Sun was on our meridian, which establishes our longitude at LAN. We find this time by finding the difference in time between that of AM-H and PM-H, and halving it. This value is then added to the GMT of AM-H to find the GMT of LAN.

The Sun's Greenwich hour angle, GHA, is then determined for the time of LAN; in West longitude, this coincides with the vessel's longitude at LAN; in East longitude, it is subtracted from 360° to give the longitude.

It may be noted here that a given error in determining the correct GMT of PM-H is halved in finding the longitude at LAN. Thus, if the error in the time of PM-H were exactly one minute, the error in the longitude at LAN would be 30 seconds, or 7.'5.

The following extreme case was prepared to illustrate the marked effect that changes in the latitude and declination can have on the PM-H. It may be of interest to note that in this example the error in the longitude determined for the time of LAN did not exceed 0.'5; in other words, the difference between the AM-H and PM-H meridian angles was less than 1.'0. Ideally, they should have been equal.

Example: On 23 September 1971 we are in the Eastern Atlantic, bound for Galway, Ireland. We are on course 045° T, at speed 21.24 knots. All times are GMT.

We propose to determine our position at LAN using equivalent AM and PM altitudes, and the Sun's altitude at LAN. We commence observing the Sun's altitude about 10-45-00, and plot the sights. We decide to use an altitude of 33° 03.'4 for AM-H, obtained at 10-50-00, at which time our DR position was L 50° 05.'8 N, λ 16° 20.'1 W, the Sun's azimuth was about 141° True, its GHA was 344° 21.'6, and the declination was N 0° 05.'8.

We note from the *Nautical Almanac* that the Sun's declination is declining at the rate of 1.'0 per hour, and realize therefore that the altitude of the PM sight will have to be adjusted for this change, as well as for our change of latitude, which is considerable on this course and speed. However, we will not calculate these corrections until we have obtained our latitude at LAN.

To determine the correction to be applied to AM-H for the change in latitude, we must determine Z as accurately as possible for the time of AM-H.

By applying our 1050 longitude to the Sun's GHA at that time, we find that the value of t is 31° 58.′5 E, and we can write Formula (1)

$$\sin Z = \frac{\cos 0° 05.′8 \times \sin 31° 58.′5}{\cos 33° 03.′4} = 0.632$$

Z, therefore, is 39° 12.′0, and its cosine is 0.775; we note this for use later.

At 1250 we begin Sun observations for LAN. During the two-minute period from 12-54-00 to 12-56-00 we obtain the highest altitudes, which, when reduced, give a latitude of 50° 37.′1 N.

We note that, in something over two hours, our latitude has increased by some 31.′3, and we can proceed to determine the corrections to be applied to the AM-H to get the equivalent PM-H.

To correct for the change of latitude, we assume that our latitude at the time of PM-H will have increased by twice the amount of the increase to LAN. This would make it 62.′6, and multiplying this by 0.775, the cosine of Z for the AM sight, we get 48.′5 as the correction for latitude. The sign will be $(-)$, because we will be farther from the Sun.

From the *Almanac*, we note that the declination decreases by 3.′9 in the four hours from GMT 1100 to 1500. To correct for this change, we write Formula (2)

$$\sin M = \frac{\cos 50° 37.′1 \times \sin 31° 58.′5}{\cos 33° 03.′4} = 0.401$$

M, therefore, is 23° 38′, and its cosine is 0.916.

We multiply the estimated decrease in declination, 3.′9, by 0.916, and obtain the correction, 3.′6, for the change in declination. Here, also, the sign will be $(-)$, because the Sun is moving away from us.

We can now apply the two corrections to obtain the equivalent PM-H

AM-H	H 33° 03.′4
Corr. for ΔL $(-)$ 48.′5	
Corr. for Δd $(-)$ 3.′6	
Net corr.	$(-)$ 52.′1
PM-H	32° 11.′3

At about 1454 we begin observing the Sun, continuing to take sights until its altitude is below 32°. These sights are plotted against time, and from the line of "best fit" we find that the Sun's PM-H was 32° 11.′3 at GMT 14-59-53.

We can now proceed to find the time the Sun was on our meridian at LAN as follows

Time of PM-H	GMT $(-)$	14-59-53
Time of AM-H	GMT	10-50-00
Difference		4-09-53
One-half difference		2-04-56
Time of AM-H	GMT $(+)$	10-50-00
Time of LAN	GMT	12-54-56
GHA Sun at	GMT	12-54-56 = 15° 36.'0

Our longitude at LAN, at GMT 12-54-36, was therefore 15° 36.'0 W; this, with the latitude we obtained at that time, 50° 37.'1 N, gives us a good approximation of our GMT 1255 position.

Latitude Approximated by Altitude of Polaris

Approximate latitude may be determined by applying two corrections to the corrected sextant altitude of Polaris.

The first, and major, correction hinges on the local hour angle of Aries, LHA Υ; this correction is given in the table below for every 10° of LHA Υ for the year 1971. Stated next to each correction is its annual change, together with the sign of the change. Although the change in the value of the correction is not linear, an approximation of the correction for nontabulated values of LHA Υ may be obtained by interpolating either by eye or by slide rule.

The second correction is an arbitrary one of $(+)$ 1.'0; it combines the mean values of the a_1 and a_2 corrections for latitudes between 10° and 50° North, and the month of the observation given in the *Nautical Almanac*.

Main Corrections for 1971 to be Applied to Corrected Sextant Altitudes to Obtain Latitude, and Annual Change in this Correction

LHA Υ	Main Corr.	Annual Δ	LHA Υ	Main Corr.	Annual Δ	LHA Υ	Main Corr.	Annual Δ	LHA Υ	Main Corr.	Annual Δ
0°	−45.'4	+0.'4	90°	−27.'6	0	180°	+43.'3	−0.'4	270°	+25.'9	0
10°	−49.'5	+0.'3	100°	−19.'4	−0.'1	190°	+47.'2	−0.'4	280°	+17.'8	+0.'1
20°	−52.'0	+0.'3	110°	−10.'7	−0.'1	200°	+49.'7	−0.'3	290°	+ 9.'2	+0.'2
30°	−53.'0	+0.'3	120°	− 1.'7	−0.'2	210°	+50.'6	−0.'3	300°	+ 0.'2	+0.'2
40°	−52.'4	+0.'2	130°	+ 7.'3	−0.'2	220°	+50.'0	−0.'3	310°	− 8.'8	+0.'2
50°	−50.'2	+0.'2	140°	+16.'0	−0.'3	230°	+47.'9	−0.'2	320°	−17.'6	+0.'3
60°	−46.'4	+0.'2	150°	+24.'2	−0.'3	240°	+44.'3	−0.'2	330°	−25.'9	+0.'3
70°	−41.'3	+0.'1	160°	+31.'6	−0.'3	250°	+39.'3	−0.'1	340°	−33.'5	+0.'3
80°	−35.'0	+0.'1	170°	+38.'0	−0.'4	260°	+33.'1	−0.'1	350°	−40.'0	+0.'3
90°	−27.'6	0	180°	+43.'3	−0.'4	270°	+25.'9	0	360°	−45.'4	+0.'4

Example: On 2 July 1974 we observed Polaris to have a corrected sextant altitude, Ho, of 37° 41.′4. Using the *Long-Term Star Almanac,* we determine the LHA ♈ to be 137° 29.′6. We wish to determine our approximate latitude.

We set the problem up as follows:

For 1971, LHA ♈ 130°, the main correction is (+) 7.′3, Annual Δ (−) 0.′2
For 1971, LHA ♈ 140°, the main correction is (+) 16.′0, Annual Δ (−) 0.′3
For 1971, $\qquad\qquad\qquad\qquad$ Δ 10° = (+) 8.′7

To find the value of the correction for 137° 29.′6, or 137.°5, we use the ratio

$$10° : (+) 8.′7 :: 7.°5 : X$$

X being the adjustment we need, or (+) 6.′5.

The correction for 137.°5 for 1971 is, therefore, (+) 13.′8 (7.′3 + 6.′5).

The annual change for LHA ♈ 130° is (−) 0.′2, for 140° it is (−) 0.′3; for 137.°5 it will therefore be (−) 0.′275. Our base year, 1971, is three years earlier than 1974; therefore 3 × (−) 0.′275 equals (−) 0.′825; we will call it (−) 0.′8.

We can now write

Correction for LHA ♈ 137.°5, 1971	(+)	13.′8
Adjustment for 1974	(−)	0.′8
Correction for LHA ♈ 137.°5, 1974	(+)	13.′0
Second correction	(+)	1.′0
Ho		37° 41.′4
Latitude		37° 55.′4 N

Reduction to the Meridian

A latitude line of position, LOP, is sometimes highly desirable, as, for example, when the Sun's declination is close to the observer's latitude so that it remains generally near East of the observer during the entire forenoon, and near West during the afternoon. Under such circumstances, the observer would be able easily to establish his longitude, but to establish his latitude, he would have to rely on an observation at local apparent noon, LAN, when the Sun transited his meridian. Should cloud cover interfere with an observation at LAN, he would, however, be able to obtain a latitude line by a reduction to his meridian, provided a Sun sight could be obtained within 28 minutes of the time of LAN; the shorter the time interval, the more accurate the results obtained. Reduction to the meridian is the process of applying a correction to an altitude observed when a body is near the celestial meridian, in order to find the equivalent meridian altitude at the time of the observation.

The following formulae are intended for use with the slide rule in obtaining the reduction to the meridian at upper transit. They will furnish a very close approximation of the true value of the correction, when the latter does not exceed 32 minutes of arc. If the correction, as calculated, exceeds 32 minutes, it may be considerably in error. The reduction should not be used in high latitudes.

The first formula is

$$A = 30.56 \tan L \, (\overset{+}{\underset{\sim}{}}) \, 30.56 \tan d \tag{1}$$

where A is a value to be used in the second formula, L is the ship's latitude by best estimate, and d is the declination. The sign is $(+)$ if L and d are of opposite name, and it is $(\sim)$ if they are of the same name.

The second formula is

$$C = \frac{t^2}{A} \tag{2}$$

where C is the correction, in minutes of arc, to be added to the observed altitude in calculating the latitude; t is the meridian angle in minutes of time; and A is the value found by Formula (1).

Example 1: In L 23° 33.′0 N by estimate, the Sun is observed 11 minutes 15 seconds after the computed time of transit to have a corrected altitude of 80° 15.′5. The Sun's declination at the instant of observation is N 14° 12.′0. We require our latitude at the time of the observation.

Using the sign ($\sim$) because L and d are of the same name, we write

$$A = 30.56 \times \tan 23° 33.′0 \sim 30.56 \times \tan 14° 12.′0 = 13.30 \sim 7.73 = 5.57$$

We can now use Formula (2), which becomes

$$C = \frac{11.25^2}{5.57} = \frac{126.5}{5.57} = 22.70$$

The correction, therefore, is $(+) 22.′7$ for C; 80° 15.′5 + 22.′7 equals 80° 38.′2, which we will use as the altitude.

Here, our latitude equals 90° $(+)$ declination $(-)$ altitude, or 90° + 14° 12.′0 − 80° 38.′2. At the time of the observation, our latitude, therefore, was 23° 33.′8 N.

Example 2: We observe the Sun 24 minutes 32 seconds after the computed time of transit to have a corrected altitude of 43° 36.′1, at which time its declination was N 11° 03.′2. Our best estimate makes our latitude 34° 58.′0 S. We require our latitude at the time of observation.

In this case, L and d are of opposite names, so Formula (1) is written

$$A = 30.56 \times \tan 34° 58.′0 + 30.56 \tan 11° 03.′2 = 21.37 + 5.97 = 27.34$$

24 minutes 32 seconds equals 24.53 minutes, so we write Formula (2)

$$C = \frac{24.53^2}{27.34} = \frac{602}{27.34} = 22.0$$

The correction to the altitude is therefore $(+) 22.′0$, making the altitude 43° 58.′1. The altitude in this instance equals 90° $(-)$ declination and $(-)$ altitude, or 90° − 11° 03.′2 − 43° 58.′1, which is 34° 58.′7.

Our latitude at the time of the observation, therefore, was 34° 58.′7 S.

Amplitudes

True amplitude is angular distance, North or South, measured from the observer's prime vertical (true East or true West) to a body centered on the celestial horizon. Amplitude observations are extremely useful for checking the compass, as the body's bearing can be obtained with maximum accuracy when on the horizon, and the formula for calculating the amplitude is extremely simple. As a general rule, amplitudes should be avoided in high latitudes.

An amplitude, being a direction measured from the prime vertical, is given the prefix E for East, if the body is rising, and W, if it is setting. It is also given a suffix, N for North, or S for South, to agree with the name of the body's declination. Amplitudes are expressed to the nearest tenth of a degree.

The body most frequently observed for the purpose of obtaining an amplitude is the Sun, although planets and stars may also be used. When the Sun's lower limb is some two-thirds of a diameter, or about 21 minutes, above the visible horizon, its center is on the celestial horizon. A planet or star is on the celestial horizon when it is about 32 minutes, or the diameter of the Sun, above the visible horizon. The Moon does not lend itself well to amplitude observations, because it is on the celestial horizon when its upper limb is on the visible horizon.

It has been the practice to convert the bearing or azimuth as observed by compass to an observed amplitude, and then to compare it with the calculated amplitude. However, many people find it simpler to obtain the deviation, or gyro error, if both amplitudes are converted to azimuths reckoned from the North, Zn, and this is the method we will use: for example, E 10.°5 S becomes Zn 100.°5 (90° + 10.°5), and W 10.°5 S becomes Zn 259.°5 (270.° − 10.°5).

The true amplitude, with the body centered on the celestial horizon, is found by the formula

$$\text{sin amplitude} = \frac{\text{sin declination}}{\text{cos latitude}}$$

Example 1: We are in DR latitude 26° 14.′0 N, and observe the setting Sun when its lower limb is about 21 minutes above the visible horizon; the declination, *d*, is S 8° 46.′4. The Sun's azimuth by magnetic compass is 273.°0, and the variation is 13.°6 W. We need the deviation on the current heading.

First, we determine the true amplitude, and convert it to azimuth. Then, we apply the variation to the azimuth obtained by compass, and compare the result to the true azimuth

$$\text{sin amplitude} = \frac{\sin d\,(8°\,46.′4)}{\cos L\,(26°\,14.′0)} = 0.1703 = \text{W } 9.°8 \text{ S} = \text{Zn } 260.°2 \text{ True}$$

True	Zn 260.°2
Variation	13.°6 W
Magnetic	Zn 273.°8
Azimuth by compass	Zn 273.°0
Deviation	0.°8 E

We, therefore, call the deviation 1° E.

If the observation is made when the body is centered on the visible horizon, a correction is required in order to refer it to the celestial horizon. A close approximation of this correction in latitudes between 0° and 50° and for declinations between 0° and 24° N or S, is given in the table below. In no instance will the error in the correction obtained from this table be greater than 0.°2; in the great majority of cases, it will not exceed 0.°1. If greater accuracy is required, Table 28 in *Bowditch* should be used.

The correction is applied to the azimuth obtained by compass in the direction *away* from the elevated pole; that is to say, for an observer in North latitude, the correction is towards the South, and vice versa.

Correction of Amplitudes for Bodies Observed Centered on the Visible Horizon for Declinations 0° to 24°

Latitude	Correction	Latitude	Correction
0°	0°	38°	0.°6
10°	0.°1	42°	0.°7
15°	0.°2	46°	0.°8
20°	0.°3	48°	0.°9
30°	0.°4	50°	1.°0
34°	0.°5		

Example 2: Our DR latitude is 33° 42.′1 S, and the Sun's declination, *d*, is S 18° 23.′6 when you observe it at sunrise, centered on the visible horizon. The Sun's azimuth by gyro is 113.°5. We need the gyro error.

As in Example 1, the first step is to determine the true amplitude and convert it to azimuth. We then take the correction from the table, apply it to the azimuth obtained by gyro, and compare the result to the true azimuth to obtain the gyro error.

$$\text{sin amplitude} = \frac{\sin d\,(18°\,23.′6)}{\cos L\,(33°\,42.′1)} = 22°\,17' = \text{true amplitude E } 22.°3 \text{ S}$$

$$= \text{Zn } 112.°3$$

Bearing by gyro	Zn 113.°5
Correction for L from table ($-$)	Zn 0.°5 N
	Zn 113.°0

observed   Zn 113.°0

gyro error   0.°7 W

Rate of Change of Altitude

It is at times desirable to determine a body's rate of change of altitude. If a sequence of sights of the same body has been taken, the rate of change provides a check on the consistency of the observations. Also, if a star finder has been used to predict altitudes and azimuths, and visibility has caused a considerable delay in obtaining sights, correction of the sextant setting will compensate for the delay.

The formula for calculating the rate of change of altitude, ΔH, in *minutes of time* is

$$\Delta H = 15 \times \cos L \sin Z \tag{1}$$

Z being the angle between the body and the meridian.

To obtain ΔH in *seconds of time,* the formula is

$$\Delta H = \frac{\cos L \times \sin Z}{4} \tag{2}$$

Example: We are in L 30°, and the predicted azimuth of a body is 100°. We want to find the rate of change of altitude in minutes of time.

Since the body's predicted azimuth is 100°, Z is 80° (180° − 100°) and Formula (1) becomes

$$\Delta H = 15 \times \cos 30° \sin 80° = 12.'8 \text{ per minute of time}$$

The rate of change of altitude, as found above, applies to a stationary observer. However, it yields acceptable results aboard vessels steaming at normal speeds.

Rate of Change of Azimuth

A stationary observer may find the rate of change of azimuth of a heavenly body by use of two formulae: the first determines the parallactic angle, M; the second provides the actual rate of change of azimuth. In the celestial triangle, PZM, the parallactic angle, M, is the one that lies at the body. To find the angle, we use the formula

$$\sin M = \frac{\cos L \times \sin Z}{\cos d} \tag{1}$$

in which L is the latitude, Z the azimuth angle, and d the declination.

Having found the angle, M, we proceed to find the rate of change of azimuth per minute of time. For this we use the formula

$$\Delta Z' = \frac{15 \times \cos d \times \cos M}{\cos H} \tag{2}$$

in which $\Delta Z'$ is the rate of change of azimuth in minutes of arc per minute of time, and H is the computed altitude or the corrected sextant altitude.

Although Formula (2) gives the rate of change of azimuth in relation to a stationary observer, the results it provides in relation to ships travelling at normal speeds are, in most cases, acceptably accurate.

Example: Our latitude is 40° N, and the declination is N 27° 30'. The azimuth, Zn, is 163.°9, which we will write as azimuth angle, 16° 06' (180° − 163° 54'), and the corrected altitude, Ho, is 77° 04.'2. We wish to determine the rate of change of azimuth in minutes of arc in one minute of time.

We write Formula (1)

$$\sin M = \frac{\cos L \, 40° \times \sin Z \, 16° 06'}{\cos d \, 27° 30'} = 0.2395 = 13° 52'$$

We next write Formula (2)

$$\Delta Z' = \frac{15 \times \cos d \, 27° 30' \times \cos M \, 13° 52'}{\cos Ho \, 77° 04.'2} = 57.'8$$

The azimuth, therefore, is changing at a rate of about 57.'8 per minute of time.

Times of Sunrise, Sunset, and Civil Twilight

Sunrise and sunset occur when the Sun's upper limb touches the horizon; under standard conditions of atmosphere and refraction, the apparent times of sunrise and sunset occur at sea level when the Sun's center is 50 minutes of arc below the visible horizon; in other words, when its altitude, H, is $(-)\,0°\,50'$. In determining the times of these phenomena by the formula given below, allowance can be made for the height of eye by numerically adding the correction for the dip of the horizon to the altitude, $(-)\,0°\,50'$. Thus, if the time of sunrise or of sunset were required for height of 100 feet, for which height of eye the correction for dip is $(-)\,9.'7$, the value used for H would be $(-)\,0°\,59.'7$. While the altitude is negative at the time of sunrise or of sunset, the $(-)$ sign is not used in the formula, which is

$$\cos t_1 = \frac{\sin H\,(\overset{+}{\underset{\sim}{}})\,(\sin L \times \sin d)}{\cos L \times \cos d} \tag{1}$$

in which t_1 is an auxiliary angle. H, the Sun's altitude, is usually assumed to be $(-)\,0°\,50'$, L is the latitude, and d the declination at about the time of the desired phenomenon.

The sign in the dividend is $(+)$ if L and d are of the same name, and $(\sim)$ if they are of opposite names.

After having found the angular value of t_1, we determine the difference in Greenwich hour angle, GHA, at about the time of the desired phenomenon, between the apparent or actual Sun and the mean Sun, in accordance with which our clocks run. Thus, if the Greenwich mean time, GMT, of the phenomenon were near 0800, and the GHA Sun at 0800 GMT were $298°\,24.'8$, we would have a difference of $1°\,35.'2\,(300° - 298°\,24.'8)$, with the apparent Sun West of, or slow on, the mean Sun. In this connection, it may be helpful to remember that the GHA mean Sun is $360°$ at GMT 1200, and $180°$ at GMT 2400.

Having found the angle between the mean Sun and the apparent Sun, we apply it to the angle t_1 in accordance with the following rules:

If the apparent Sun is West of, or slow on, the mean Sun, the angle found above is subtracted from t_1;

If the apparent Sun is East of, or fast on, the mean Sun, the angle found above is added to t_1.

Having thus corrected t_1, we proceed as follows for sunrise:

If sunrise is before 0600 local mean time, LMT, we use the angle as found above;

If sunrise is after 0600 LMT, we subtract this angle from 180°.

For sunset, the rules are:

If sunset is before 1800 LMT, we add 180° to the angle;

If sunset is after 1800 LMT, we subtract the angle from 360°.

If, at this point, we converted into time the corrected angle thus found, we would have the LMT of the phenomenon. However, we are interested in clock or zone time, so we next find the angular difference between our longitude and that of the central meridian of the time zone we are using. This we add to the angle if we are West of zone meridian, and subtract if we are East of it.

The last step is to convert into time the angle we have found; this gives us the time of the phenomenon.

Example 1: Our position is L 40°01.'3 N, λ 70°50.'7 W. The date is 30 March 1971, our clocks are set to Zone (+) 5 time, and we wish to determine the time of sunrise, which we know will occur somewhat before 0600 LMT.

Our first step is to determine the Sun's declination at or near the time of sunrise. From the almanac, we find that at 0600 our time (GMT 1100) it will be N 3°36.'4. We can now write Formula (1) as

$$\cos t_1 = \frac{\sin 0° 50' + (\sin 40° 01.'3 \times \sin 3° 36.'4)}{\cos 40° 01.'3 \times \cos 3° 36.'4}$$

the sign in the dividend being (+) because the latitude and declination are of the same name. This formula may now be rewritten

$$\cos t_1 = \frac{0.01455 + 0.0405}{0.764} = \frac{0.05505}{0.764} = 0.0720 = 85° 52.'0$$

t_1 is, therefore, 85°52.'0.

We next find the angular difference in hour angle between the apparent Sun and the mean Sun.

At GMT 1100, the GHA of the apparent Sun is $343°49.'5$, while the GHA of the mean Sun is $345°00.'0$. The apparent Sun is, therefore, East of, or slow by, $1°10.'5$; this will, therefore, be added to t_1

$$\begin{array}{ll} t_1 & 85°52.'0 \\ (+) & 1°10.'5 \\ \hline & 87°02.'5 \end{array}$$

In this instance, the sign is $(+)$ because the apparent Sun is East of the mean Sun. Furthermore, since we expect sunrise to occur before 0600, we can proceed directly with the angle we now have.

Our clocks are set to zone $(+)$ 5 time. Consequently, the central meridian of our zone is $75°$ W and our longitude is $70°50.'7$ W. We are therefore $4°09.'3$ East of, or fast on, the zone meridian, and our sunrise will occur before it does at $\lambda\ 75°$ W. This angle, $4°09.'3$ will, therefore, be subtracted from the angle found above

$$\begin{array}{ll} & 87°02.'5 \\ (-) & 4°09.'3 \\ \hline & 82°53.'2 \end{array}$$

Converted to time, $82°53.'2$ gives us 05 hours 31 minutes 33 seconds.

We would, therefore, call the clock time of sunrise 0532 to the nearest minute, Zone $(+)$ 5 time.

Example 2: On 14 May 1971, at 1700 $(+)$ 3 time we are in L $22°34.'0$ S, $\lambda\ 45°37.'0$ W, and we wish to determine the time of sunset, which we know will occur before 1800 LMT.

From the almanac, we find the Sun's declination at GMT 2000 to be N $18°37.'2$. The sign in the dividend is $(\sim)$ because latitude and declination are of opposite names, and Formula (1) becomes

$$\cos t_1 = \frac{\sin 0°50' \sim (\sin 22°34.'0 \times \sin 18°37.'2)}{\cos 22°34.'0 \times \cos 18°37.'2} = \frac{0.01455 \sim 0.1225}{0.875}$$

$$= \frac{0.10795}{0.875} = 0.1233 = 82°55.'0$$

t_1, therefore, is $82°55.'0$.

At GMT 2000 we find the Sun's GHA to be $120°55.'7$, while the GHA of the mean Sun is $120°00.'0$. Therefore, the apparent Sun is $0°55.'7$ West of the mean Sun, and we will subtract this angle from t_1

$$t_1 \quad 82°\,55.'0$$
$$(-) \quad 0°\,55.'7$$
$$81°\,59.'3$$

We know that sunset will occur before 1800, so we add 180° to this angle

$$81°\,59.'3$$
$$(+)\; 180°\,00.'0$$
$$261°\,59.'3$$

Our clocks are set ($+$) 3 time; the central meridian for this zone is 45° W. However, our longitude is 45° 37.'0 W, so we are 0° 37.'0 West of the zone meridian, and our sunset will occur later than it will at the zone meridian. We will, therefore, add the 0° 37.'0

$$261°\,59.'3$$
$$(+) \qquad 37.'0$$
$$262°\,36.'3$$

Converted to time, 262° 36.'3 is 17 hours 30 minutes 25 seconds.

Since it is customary to work to the nearest minute, we would state the time of our sunset as 1730 ($+$) 3 time.

It is practicable to determine separately the times of sunrise or sunset and the times of the beginning or ending of the corresponding periods of civil or other twilight. However, in ordinary practice, the navigator requires the time of both sunrise or sunset and of its corresponding civil twilight. Since the formula used in determining the times of both phenomena is the same, except for one factor, it saves effort if the computations are combined.

Civil twilight begins in the morning, when the Sun is 6° below the horizon, and ends at sunrise. Conversely, it begins at sunset and ends when the Sun is again 6° below the horizon. The darker period of civil twilight is used by the navigator to observe stars; its determination is therefore of interest to him. However, he may be able to obtain some star sights when the Sun is somewhat more than 6° below the horizon.

Nautical twilight begins when the Sun is 12° below the horizon, and astronomical twilight begins when it is 18° below the horizon. The formula for finding apparent time of the beginning or end of civil twilight is the same as that used for determining the times of sunrise and sunset, except that the altitude, H, ($-$) 6° is substituted for H ($-$) 0° 50$'$. Should the time of nautical or astronomical twilight be required, 12° or 18°, respectively, are used in the formula instead of 6°. The times thus found may be converted to zone times.

As with the times of sunrise and sunset, the value read from the slide rule

111

for t_1 may represent the actual angle t, or its supplement. The determination of which to use in obtaining the LMT of the phenomenon is discussed below. The LMT must finally be converted to clock time.

The value of t_1 for civil twilight may be found by the formula

$$\cos t_1 = \frac{\sin H \,(\overset{+}{\sim})\, 6°0' \sim (\sin L \sin d)}{\cos L \cos d} \tag{2}$$

where L is the latitude, and d the declination.

The sign in the dividend is $(+)$ if L and d are of the same name, and $(\sim)$ if they are of opposite names.

Having found the angular value of t_1, we would proceed to find the equivalent ship's time of the phenomenon, in the manner described above for finding the time of sunrise or sunset.

However, once the time of sunrise or sunset has been obtained, it is simpler to find the angular difference between the t_1 for sunrise or sunset, and the t_1 for civil twilight. This difference converted directly to time is subtracted from the time of sunrise to obtain the time of the start of civil twilight in the morning, and is added to the time of sunset to obtain the time of the end of civil twilight in the evening.

Thus, in Example 1 above, on finding the time of sunrise in L 40°01.'3 N, λ 70°50.'7 W on 30 March 1971, the formula for finding t_1 was written

$$\cos t_1 = \frac{\sin 0°\,50' + (\sin 40°01.'3 \times \sin 3°\,36.'4)}{\cos 40°01.'3 \times \cos 3°\,36.'4} = \frac{0.01455 + 0.0405}{0.764}$$
$$= 85°\,52.'0$$

We would substitute $\sin H\,6°$ for $\sin H\,0°\,50'$ and write

$$\cos t_1 = \frac{0.1045 + 0.0405}{0.764} = \frac{0.145}{0.764} = 0.1898 = 79°\,04.'0$$

The difference between the first t_1, $85°\,52.'0$, and this t_1, $79°\,04.'0$, is found to be $6°\,48.'0$. This difference converted to time proves to be 27 minutes to the nearest minute. Sunrise, we found, would come at 0532 $(+5)$.

Civil twilight, therefore, would start 27 minutes earlier, or at 0505.

Similarly, in Example (2) above, we wished to find the time of sunset on 14 May 1971 for L 22°34.'0 S, λ 45°37.'0 W.

The formula for t_1 was written

$$\cos t_1 = \frac{0.01455 \sim 0.1225}{0.875} = 82°\,55.'0$$

given a zone time of sunset of 1730.

We would rewrite it as

$$\cos t_1 = \frac{0.1045 \sim 0.1225}{0.875} = \frac{0.0180}{0.875} = 0.02056 = 88°\,49.'3$$

The difference between $88°\,49.'3$ and $82°\,55.'0$ is $5°\,54.'3$; converted to the nearest minute of time, it becomes 24 minutes.

Civil twilight would, therefore, end at 1754, zone $(+)$ 3 time $(1730 + 24$ minutes$)$.

Times of Moonrise and Moonset

In the Navy, particularly, the times of moonrise and moonset are of interest. The *Nautical Almanac* tabulates these times for selected latitudes for every day, and includes interpolation tables to correct for the ship's latitude and longitude.

However, interpolation can be made both faster and more accurately with the slide rule than with the interpolation tables. For example, let us assume that we want to find the time of moonrise on the night of 14 August 1971, and that our position is L 43° 24.′5 N, λ 63° 27.′5 W. For daylight-saving purposes, our clocks are set to Zone ($+$) 3 time.

The first step is to interpolate for latitude. The *Almanac* tabulates moonrise for L 40° N as 23-24, and for L 45° N as 23-03; the difference therefore for 5° is ($-$) 21 minutes, and our DR latitude is 3.°4 North of L 40° N. By ratio then

$$5°: (-)\ 21\ m :: 3.°4 : (-)\ 14.3\ m, \text{ or } (-)\ 14.3 \text{ minutes}$$

so the time of moonrise for our latitude and λ 0° is 23-09.7 (2324 − 14.3).

The next step is to interpolate for our longitude. Since we are in *West longitude,* we find the time of moonrise for our latitude for the *following day;* if we were in *East longitude,* we would find the time of moonrise for our latitude for the *preceding day.* For 15 August, the *Almanac* tabulates the time of moonrise in L 40° N as 24-19 (in other words 0019 on the 16th), and for L 45° N, 23-57 is tabulated. Using the same ratio form as before, we write

$$5°: (-)\ 22\ m :: 3.°4 : (-)\ 14.95\ m, \text{ or } (-)\ 15.0 \text{ minutes}$$

so the time of moonrise for our latitude and 0° λ on the following day (actually the 16th) is 24-04.

The difference in the time of moonrise in 24 hours, or 360°, at our latitude is therefore (+) 54 minutes (24-04 − 23-10). Our longitude is 63°27.′5 W, or 63.°46 W, so we write

$$\frac{63.°46}{360°} \times (+) 54 \text{ m} = (+) 9.52 \text{ m}$$

so moonrise on 14 August at our position will come at 23-19.22 (23-09.7 + 9.52), or at 23 hours 19 minutes 13 seconds, local mean time, LMT, which we must convert to zone time.

Our clocks are set to zone (+) 3 time, and the central meridian of this zone is 45° W. Our longitude is 63°27.′5 W, so we are 18°27.′5 West of the 45th meridian. This converted to time is 1 hour 13 minutes 50 seconds, and because we are West of the 45th merdian it is added to the LMT of moonrise

$$
\begin{array}{lll}
\text{LMT} & 23 \text{ h } 19 \text{ m } 13 \text{ s} \\
(+) \quad \lambda\text{W} & \underline{1 \text{ h } 13 \text{ m } 50 \text{ s}} \\
& 24 \text{ h } 33 \text{ m } 03 \text{ s}
\end{array}
$$

The Moon, therefore, will rise at 00-33-03, 15 August, (+) 3 time, which we would call 00-33.

Aboard a fast moving vessel, it is sometimes necessary to make a second determination of the time of the phenomenon, because the predicted DR position at the time found may be distant from the DR used to obtain the first determination.

Thus, the navigator might have used his expected DR at 22-00 to find the time of moonrise, but he finds that it will occur at 23-00 at that position. In such a case, he would rework the problem, using his 23-00 position to obtain a second estimate of the time of moonrise.

Celestial Observations

Time and Altitude on the Prime Vertical

Sometimes, as when working a time sight or when it is necessary to know the longitude, it is desirable to obtain an observation on the prime vertical.

It must be borne in mind that a body with a declination having a name opposite to that of the latitude of the observer, will not cross the latter's prime vertical above the horizon: its nearest approaches while visible will be at the times of rising and setting. A body having a declination of the same name as the latitude of the observer, but numerically greater, will not cross the prime vertical. However, a body having a declination of the same name as the observer's latitude, but smaller numerically, will cross his prime vertical above the horizon. At each crossing, the meridian angles and altitudes are equal; the meridian angles are always less than 90°.

The meridian angle, t, of a body on the prime vertical may be found by means of the formula

$$\cos t = \tan d \times \cot L \qquad (1)$$

where d is the declination, and L the latitude. When working with the slide rule, if L is less than 45°, it may be simpler to write the formula as

$$\cos t = \frac{\tan d}{\tan L} \qquad (2)$$

The altitude of a body, H, when it is on the prime vertical, may be found by means of the formula

$$\sin H = \frac{\sin d}{\sin L} \qquad (3)$$

With these formulae, it is possible to determine the approximate time when a body will be on the prime vertical, and its altitude at that moment.

Where a body's declination is of the same name as, but numerically greater than, the observer's latitude, its meridian angle at the moment of nearest approach to the prime vertical may be found by the formula

$$\cos t = \frac{1}{\tan d \cot L} \tag{4}$$

or, if more convenient

$$\cos t = \frac{\tan L}{\tan d} \tag{5}$$

Its altitude at this moment is found by the formula

$$\sin H = \frac{\sin L}{\sin d} \tag{6}$$

Its approximate azimuth angle, Z, at this moment may be found by the formula

$$\sin Z = \frac{\cos d \sin t}{\cos H} \tag{7}$$

Example 1: We are in L 51° 25.'0 N, λ 47° 41.'0 W, and the Sun bears slightly North of East; its declination is N 21° 49.'8. We wish to observe the Sun on the prime vertical, and to know the approximate time when it will be on the prime vertical and its approximate altitude at that moment.

We first solve for *t*, by writing Formula (1)

$$\cos t = \tan 21° 49.'8 \times \cot 51° 25.'0 = .3196$$

The meridian angle, therefore, is 71° 22' E.

We then apply our longitude to find the Sun's angular position relative to the meridian of Greenwich when its *t* is 71° 22' E

$$
\begin{array}{l}
t\text{E } 71° 22' \\
\lambda\text{W } 47° 41' \\
\hline
 23° 41'
\end{array}
$$

The Sun's angular distance East of Greenwich when it is on our prime vertical is, therefore, 23° 41', which converts to 1 hour 34 minutes 44 seconds.

If we are willing to assume that the Sun transits Greenwich at noon GMT, the GMT of our prime vertical sight would be about 10-25 (12-00 − 1-35). A closer approximation may be found by determining the Greenwich hour angle, GHA, of the Sun, 336° 19' (360° − 23° 41'), then noting from the *Nautical Almanac* the GMT of this GHA. If the ship's time is required, it is necessary only to apply, with sign reversed, the zone description to which the ship's clocks are set, to the GMT.

To find the altitude of the Sun when it is on our prime vertical, we use Formula (3), which, if the Sun's declination has not changed, becomes

$$\sin H = \frac{\sin 21°49.'8}{\sin 51°25'} = 0.476$$

When the Sun is on our prime vertical, its altitude will, therefore, be about 28°25′.

Example 2: We are in L 10°09.'6 N, and the Sun's declination is N 19°30.'1. We wish to determine the meridian angle, altitude, and azimuth of the Sun at its nearest morning approach to our prime vertical.

We first find the meridian angle by Formula (5), which here will be

$$\cos t = \frac{\tan 10°09.'6}{\tan 19°30.'1} = 0.506$$

The meridian angle, therefore, is approximately 59°38.'0, and is named East.

We next find the altitude, using Formula (6), which we write

$$\sin H = \frac{\sin 10°09.'6}{\sin 19°30.'1} = 0.528$$

The approximate altitude at this moment is, therefore, 31°52.'0.
The approximate azimuth we find by using Formula (7)

$$\sin Z = \frac{\cos 19°30.'1 \times \sin 59°38.'0}{\cos 31°52.'0} = 0.957$$

The azimuth angle, therefore, is about N 73°10′ E, which would make the azimuth approximately 073.°2.

Line-Of-Position Bisectors

A constant, but unknown, error may affect all celestial observations. When such an error, which may be caused by abnormal refraction, exists and the observed bodies are not well distributed in azimuth, the fix may not lie at the center of the polygon formed by the plotted lines of position, as one would ordinarily assume: it may be an *exterior fix,* that is, a fix lying outside the polygon.

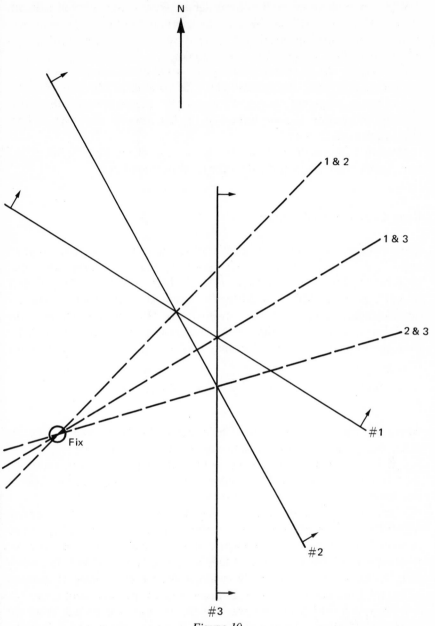

Figure 10
Line-of-Position Bisectors to Determine the Position of the Fix

When three or more bodies are observed lying within 180° of azimuth of each other, it is wise to use bisectors to determine the fix. The angle formed by each pair of lines of position is bisected by a line drawn in the direction of the *mean of the azimuths* of the two bodies.

For example, let us assume that due to partial cloud cover, we were able to observe only three stars at twilight. The azimuth of star #1 was 030°, that of star #2 was 060°, and of #3 it was 090°. Figure 10 shows the resulting lines of position as solid lines, and the bisectors for each pair of lines of position as dashed lines.

Note that the resulting fix at the intersection of the three bisectors lies well outside the triangle formed by the three position lines.

Error Caused by Timing Error

An error in the timing of a celestial observation will obviously cause an error in the location of the line of position, LOP, developed from that observation. Let us first consider a single LOP, which will give a most probable position, MPP; the MPP is determined by the point at which a perpendicular, dropped from our estimated or DR position, intersects the LOP. For a given error in time of the observation, the distance of the MPP from the estimated position, EP, may be found by means of the formula

$$D = \frac{E}{4} \times \cos L \times \sin Z$$

where D is the distance in nautical miles caused by the error, E is the error in seconds of time, L is the latitude, and Z is the azimuth angle.

For a given error of one second in time, the maximum error, expressed as distance, will occur on the equator, with the body bearing due East or due West, in which case it will be 0.25 miles.

It must be borne in mind that, in this case, the error referred to involves an MPP derived from a single observation. Where a fix, obtained from two or more LOPs is involved, the position of the fix itself is in error; the error in placement of the component LOPs need not be considered. In such a case the fix will be in error only in longitude, the error being 15 minutes of arc for 1 minute of time, or 0.25 minutes of arc per second of time.

If the watch used for timing was fast the error in position will be to the West, and MPP must be moved to the East; conversely, if it was slow, the error will be to the East.

Example: A single observation of the Sun has been reduced, our DR being L 27° 43.′5 N. It was subsequently found that the stopwatch used for timing the observation had been started on chronometer time, which was 23 seconds slow. What adjustment should we make to the MPP, if the azimuth was 263.°2?

Here Z will be S 83° 12′ W (263.°2 − 180°), and the above formula will be

$$D = \frac{23}{4} \times \cos L\ 27°43.′5 \times \sin 83°12′ = 5.05 \text{ miles}$$

The MPP, therefore, should be moved 5.05 miles to the West.

Alternatively, the sight could be replotted. The watch error was 23 seconds; this, converted to longitude, equals 5.′75. The assumed or DR position from which the sight was originally plotted would, therefore, be moved 5.′75 to the West, the watch being slow on GMT.

Star Identification

The navigational stars and planets may be identified by the use of four simple formulae, found in H.O. Publication No. 211 and modified for use with sines and cosines and the slide rule. Given the body's corrected sextant altitude and true azimuth, both the declination and meridian angle may be found. Because the azimuth must be determined by observation, the best results are obtained when bodies are situated at low altitudes.

In these formulae, R and K are auxiliary angles introduced to facilitate solution; Ho is the corrected sextant altitude; Z is the true azimuth reckoned East or West from the elevated pole; L is the latitude; d is the declination; and t is the meridian angle.

$$\sin R = \sin Z \times \cos Ho \tag{1}$$

$$\sin K = \frac{\sin Ho}{\cos R} \tag{2}$$

$$\sin d = \cos R \times \cos (K \sim L) \tag{3}$$

$$\sin t = \frac{\sin R}{\cos d} \tag{4}$$

The following rules apply:

a) K takes the same name as the latitude.
b) When Z is greater than 90°, K is greater than 90°.

c) *d* is same name as L, except when Z and (K ∼ L) are both greater than 90°.

d) (K ∼ L) represents the algebraic difference between K and L; that is to say, the smaller is subtracted from the larger.

e) *t* is less than 90° when K is greater than L; conversely, it is greater than 90° when L is greater than K.

In most instances, it will not be necessary to solve for *t*, since a bright star can usually be identified by its declination.

Given the value of *t*, the local hour angle of Aries, LHA ♈, must be determined for the time of the observation; this is done by extracting the Greenwich hour angle, GHA Aries, from the almanac, and then applying the ship's longitude. If the star is to the Eastward, its *t* is converted to LHA and compared with the LHA Aries to obtain its sidereal hour angle, SHA, as shown in the example.

Note: Because it is difficult to obtain accurate azimuths, both the declination and the meridian angle obtained by this method may be considerably in error. However, no difficulty should be encountered in identifying a major navigational star, even if its calculated azimuth and meridian angle are in error by a degree or more.

Example: At Greenwich mean time, GMT, 23-59-56, 2 May 1970, in L 45° 02.′0 N, λ 60° 28.′5 W, a bright star is observed to have a corrected altitude of 10° 05.′5, and a true azimuth of 044°. We wish to identify the star.

Formula (1) becomes

$$\sin R = \sin 44° \times \cos 10° 05.′5 \therefore R = 43° 10.′0$$

Formula (2) then becomes

$$\sin K = \frac{\sin 10° 05.′5}{\cos 43° 10.′0} \therefore K = 13° 54.′0$$

which will be named North.

Having calculated K, 13° 54.′0, we obtain (K ∼ L) by subtracting 13° 54.′0 from the latitude, 45° 02.′0, (K ∼ L) therefore is 31° 08.′0. We can now write Formula (3)

$$\sin d = \cos 43° 10.′0 \times \cos 31° 08.′0 = N 38° 40.′0$$

Rule (c), above, is invoked to determine the name of the declination.

This should ordinarily be sufficient to allow us to consult the almanac and identify the star as Vega. However, to make sure of the identification, we will proceed to find *t*.

We solve for t by Formula (4)

$$\sin tE = \frac{\sin 43°10.'0}{\cos 38°40.'0} = 61°10.'0 \therefore t = 118°50.'0 \text{ E}$$

See Rule (e) above – t is greater than 90°.

Having obtained the star's meridian angle, we use the almanac to find its SHA.

	D	M
GHA Aries, GMT 2300, 2 May	205	26.3
Increment 59 m 56 sec	15	01.5
GHA Aries at time of sight	220	27.8
Longitude West	60	28.5
LHA Aries	159	59.3
Star's t 118°50.'0 E = LHA (W)	241	10.0
Difference	81	10.7 = SHA

We now have obtained a declination of N 38°40.'0, and an SHA of 81°10.'7. By referring to the list of primary navigational stars given in the daily pages of the *Nautical Almanac,* we find that Vega has a declination of N 38°44.'9, and an SHA of 81°00.'7.

Our star must, therefore, be Vega.

This method works equally well in identifying a planet. The declination is determined as above, and having found t, the meridian angle, it is combined with the vessel's longitude to determine the Greenwich hour angle of the planet. With the declination and the GHA determined, the planet may readily be identified from the almanac.

Interpolating in H.O. Publications Nos. 214 and 229

Altitudes tabulated in H.O. Publications Nos. 214 and 229 must be corrected for the difference between the actual declination and the declination assumed when entering the tables. In H.O. 214 a correction factor, called "Δd," is provided for this purpose, and at the back of each volume there is a two-part multiplication table which facilitates determination of the value of the correction. When the actual declination differs from the assumed declination by both whole minutes and tenths of minutes, it is necessary to enter the portion of the table that is devoted to whole minutes, and then the portion that covers tenths of minutes. The two products must then be added together to obtain the correction that must be applied to the tabulated altitude.

This correction may be obtained more expeditiously, and in some instances more accurately, by use of the slide rule: multiply the difference between the actual number of minutes and the number used in entering the tables by the Δd factor, then read off the correction factor to the nearest tenth of a minute.

Example 1: We have entered H.O. 214 with L 36° N, declination N 10°, and the meridian angle 19° E; the actual declination is N 10° 14.'4. We find the tabulated altitude to be 58° 48.'2, and the Δd factor to be .86.

We multiply 14.'4 (the difference between the true and assumed declination) by 0.86 by slide rule, and obtain a correction of 12.'4 (to the nearest tenth) to apply to the tabulated altitude.

Now let us obtain the correction by means of the multiplication tables in the back of H.O. 214.

$$
\begin{aligned}
\text{We find that} \quad & 14' \times .86 = 12.'0 \\
\text{and that} \quad & 0.'4 \times .86 = \underline{0.'3} \\
\text{giving a total correction of} \quad & 12.'3
\end{aligned}
$$

In this instance, the correction obtained by tables not only took longer to solve, but it was not as accurate as that obtained by slide rule.

When H.O. 214 is to be used for reducing a sight from a DR, rather than an assumed, position, it is necessary to correct the tabulated altitude for the increment of meridian angle over the tabulated value, Δt, and for the increment of the DR latitude over the whole degree used for entering the tables, in addition to the usual Δd correction.

The Δt correction factor is tabulated, and the correction for the increment of meridian angle may easily and accurately be determined with the slide rule in the same manner the Δd correction is found.

However, H.O. 214 does not tabulate a correction for an increment of latitude over the tabulated degree. This correction, which we will call ΔL, is usually found by determining the difference in the tabulated altitude for the latitude used in entering the table, and the tabulated altitude for the next greater degree of latitude, using the same values of declination and meridian angle, and then interpolating.

Example 2: Our DR position is L 24° 27.'8 N, λ 57° 16.'3 W. We obtained an afternoon observation of the Sun, which had a corrected altitude of 48° 02.'6. Its declination was S 12° 17.'8 at the time of the observation. We wish to reduce the sight from our DR position, using H.O. 214. Having applied our DR λ to the Greenwich hour angle, GHA, of the Sun, we obtain a meridian angle, t, of 20° 46.'8 W.

We enter H.O. 214 with L 24°, declination, d, 12° of contrary name, and

t 20°, extract the tabulated altitude, ht, Δd and Δt corrections as noted below, and determine the values of the corrections by slide rule

$$ht \quad 49°\,02.'2$$

Δd 0.88 × (−) 17.'8 = (−) 15.'7
Δt 0.48 × (−) 46.'8 = (−) 22.'5
Net. corr. for Δd and Δt (−) 38.'2
ht for L 24°, corrected   −38.'2
          computed altitude, Hc = $\overline{48°\,24.'0}$

We now find the difference in ht for our DR latitude

L 24° N, d S 12°, t 20° ht 49° 02.'2
L 25° N, d S 12°, t 20° ht 48° 10.'4
Difference   (−) $\overline{51.'8}$

The increment of latitude of our DR position over the base latitude of 24° is 27.'8. Then

$$(-)\,\frac{51.'8}{60'} \times 27.'8 = (-)\,24.'0$$

Therefore, our Hc 48° 24.'0 for L 24°, and corrected for Δd and Δt is decreased by this amount

          Hc 48° 24.'0
Correction for L (−)   24.'0
          Hc $\overline{48°\,00.'0}$
          Ho 48° 02.'6
     Intercept, a $\overline{2.'6}$ Towards

Having found the intercept, we interpolate by eye to determine the azimuth. For L 24° N, d (about) S 12° 15′, and t (about) 20° 45′, we see the azimuth will be 148.°5. The tabulated azimuth for L 24° N, d S 12°, and t 20° is 149.°3, and for L 25°, with the same values of d and t it is 149.°9. Since for 1° of latitude the azimuth increases 1.°6, for 27.'6 it will increase 0.°3.

The azimuth therefore is N 148.°8 W (148.°5 + 0.°3), making the Zn 211.°2 (360° − 148.°8).

Aquino Method — Fix by Observations of a Single Body

When and if there is available instrumentation that will permit azimuth to be obtained to the same degree of accuracy with which altitude can be measured by means of the sextant, we will be able to calculate both our

125

latitude and longitude by means of simultaneous altitude and azimuth observations of a celestial body.

A simple method of obtaining a fix in this manner was suggested in the 1930s by Radler de Aquino, a Brazilian naval officer and mathematician. Solution is by three simple formulae, given below. Meridian angle is found first, and converted to longitude; then latitude is found by two additional formulae.

The first formula is

$$\sin t = \frac{\cos Ho \times \sin Z}{\cos d} \tag{1}$$

where t is the meridian angle, Ho is the corrected sextant altitude, Z is the observed azimuth angle, and d is the declination. The meridian angle is then converted to local hour angle, LHA, and the longitude will equal the body's Greenwich hour angle, GHA, less the LHA.

The first formula for the latitude solution is

$$\cot A = \frac{\tan Ho}{\cos Z} \tag{2}$$

In this and the following formula, A and B represent auxiliary angles. In connection with Formula (3), remember that the cotangent of an angle equals the tangent of the complement of that angle.

The second latitude formula is

$$\tan B = \frac{\tan d}{\cos t} \tag{3}$$

If latitude and declination are of the same name, A and B are added together; if they are of opposite name, the smaller is subtracted from the larger.

Example: In DR latitude 50° N we obtain a simultaneous altitude and azimuth of the star Deneb, Ho being 83°07.′4, and Zn being 133°49.′9. Deneb's GHA was 39°27.′3, and the declination N 45°10.′3. We require our position.

The body's azimuth angle, Z, is 46°10.′1 (180° − 133°49.′9), so Formula (1) becomes

$$\sin t = \frac{\cos Ho\ 83°07.′4 \times \sin Z\ 46°10.′1}{\cos d\ 45°10.′3} = 0.1225$$

The meridian angle, therefore, is 7°02′ E, which makes the LHA 352°58′. We now find our longitude by subtracting the LHA from the star's GHA

$$
\begin{array}{ccc}
 & D & M \\
\text{GHA} & 39 & 27.3 \\
(+) & 360 & 00.0 \\
\hline
 & 399 & 27.3 \\
\text{LHA} \;(-) & 352 & 58.0 \\
\hline
\lambda & 46 & 29.3 \text{ W}
\end{array}
$$

To find the latitude, we write Formula (2) with Formula (3) below it

$$\cot A = \frac{\tan Ho\ 83°07.'4}{\cos Z\ 46°10.'1} = 11.97 = A \qquad 4°46.'5$$

$$(+)$$

$$\tan B = \frac{\tan d\ 45°10.'3}{\cos t\ 7°02.'0} = 1.014 = \begin{array}{cc} B & 45°25.'0 \\ \hline L & 50°11.'5 \text{ N} \end{array}$$

Our latitude, therefore, is 50°11.'5 N, and our longitude is 46°29.'3 W. In this case, B was added to A, since latitude and declination were of the same name.

This example lent itself well to solution by slide rule, because the altitude was great, and the observed azimuth angle, Z, was near 45°. A more rigorous solution yields a meridian angle, t, of 7°02.'2, an auxiliary angle, A, of 4°46.'2, and an auxiliary angle, B, of 45°23.'3. These figures give a latitude of 50°09.'5 N, and a longitude of 46°29.'5 W.

Willis Method — Fix by Observations of a Single Body

Another method of obtaining a fix by observation of a single body was suggested by Edward J. Willis. This method hinges on the rate of change of altitude of a body and its actual altitude at a point midway in time between the first and third observations. For best results, the time span for the three observations should be about 4 seconds (1 minute of meridian angle), and the altitudes should be obtained to an accuracy of better than a thousandth of a minute of arc. However, fair results can be obtained if the interval of time between the first and third observations is 8 minutes, or 120 minutes of arc, and the altitudes are obtained to the nearest tenth of a minute of arc.

The Willis method unfortunately does not lend itself well to solution by slide rule; it is included herein primarily as a matter of professional interest to the navigator.

The first step in this method is to find the rate of change of altitude of the body, ΔH. ΔH divided by the difference in time between the first and third observations, expressed in minutes of arc, Δt, gives the sine of an auxiliary angle, N, as shown in the following formula

$$\sin N = \frac{\Delta H}{\Delta t} \tag{1}$$

Having found the angle N, we proceed to find our latitude by means of the formula:

$$\sin L = \cos N \times \cos \left[Ho \pm \sin^{-1} \left(\frac{\sin d}{\cos N}\right)\right] \tag{2}$$

In this formula, Ho is the corrected sextant altitude of the body, obtained exactly half-way between the first and third observations; $\sin^{-1}$ indicates that $\sin d$ divided by $\cos N$ represents the sine of an angle; and d is the declination of the body. The sign following Ho is $(-)$ when L is of the same name and greater than the declination. When d is of the same name, and considerably greater than L, the angle represented by $\sin^{-1} \left(\dfrac{\sin d}{\cos N}\right)$ may be greater than 90°.

Having found our latitude, we can proceed to find the body's meridian angle, t, by the formula

$$\sin t = \frac{\sin N \times \cos Ho}{\cos d \times \cos L} \tag{3}$$

The meridian angle is then converted to local hour angle, LHA, and the longitude is found by subtracting the LHA from the Greenwich hour angle, GHA, of the body at the instant of the second sight, Ho.

This method should not be used when the body is near the observer's meridian, and it must be borne in mind that the second observation, termed Ho above, must be a separate observation, and not half the sum of the first and third altitude observations.

Example: To illustrate this method, three altitudes, H_1, Ho, and H_3, have been extracted from Volume III of H.O. Publication No. 214 for L 26° and a d of 16°, d having the same name as L, which we will assume is North. These altitudes are for three successive degrees of meridian angle, 14°, 13°, and 12°; in other words, we assume that we have obtained them exactly four minutes apart, and that they were morning Sun sights. In actual practice, all three sextant altitudes would have been corrected.

$$
\begin{array}{ll}
H_1 \;\; 75°00.'0 & \\
H_3 \;\; 73°33.'9 & \qquad Ho \;\; 74°17.'6 \\
\overline{\Delta H \;\; 1°26.'1 = 86.'1} &
\end{array}
$$

We can now find the value of the angle N by writing Formula (1)

$$\sin N = \frac{86.'1}{120'} = 0.717 = 45°\,50'$$

The value of N is, therefore, 45° 50'. We can now proceed to find the latitude, using Formula (2), which becomes

$$\sin L = \cos 45°\,50' \times \cos \left[74°\,17.'6\,(-)\sin^{-1}\left(\frac{\sin 16°}{\cos 45°\,50'} \right) \right]$$
$$= \cos 45°\,50' \times \cos [74°\,17.'6\,(-)\,23°\,18.'0]$$
$$= \cos 45°\,50' \times \cos 50°\,59.'6$$
$$= 0.438$$
$$= 25°\,58'$$

Our latitude is, therefore, 25° 58' N, and we can proceed to find the meridian angle, using Formula (3)

$$\sin t = \frac{\sin N\ 45°50' \times \cos Ho\ 74°17.'6}{\cos d\ 16° \times \cos L\ 25°58'} = 0.2248 = 12°\,59'$$

The meridian angle is therefore 12° 59' E, which we would convert to LHA and subtract from the Sun's GHA to find our longitude. In fact, a more rigorous solution yields a meridian angle of 13°, and a latitude of 26°.

These observation reductions are better than the slide rule would usually produce: to obtain them, a comparatively low latitude, low declination, and low altitudes were selected, in order to give N a value near 45°.

Fix by Two Observations Without Plotting

In an emergency, the coordinates of a fix, obtained from observations of two celestial bodies, may be determined without plotting, although the process is not as simple as plotting. For accuracy, the azimuths of the two bodies should be as nearly as possible at right angles.

The procedure is to reduce the first sight, using a DR, or preferably, an estimated position, EP. Having obtained the intercept, *a*, and azimuth, the most probable position, MPP, based on the first observation, is determined. The MPP lies at the end of the intercept; its latitude and longitude are calculated by mid-latitude sailing, using, for the course, the azimuth, or coazimuth, according to the direction of the intercept, and, for the distance, the length of the intercept.

The second observation is then reduced, using the latitude and longitude of the MPP, and the second azimuth and intercept are found. The angular

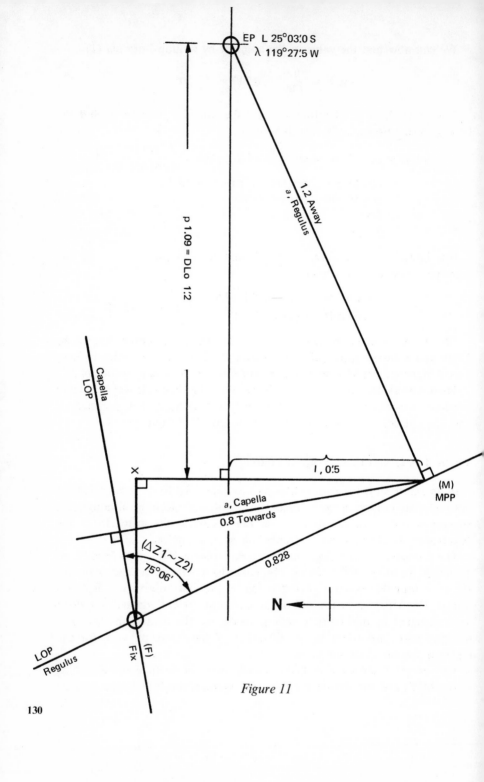

EP L 25°03′.0 S
λ 119°27′.5 W

p 1.09 = DLo 1′.2

1.2 Away
a, Regulus

Capella
LOP

×

I, 0′.5

(M)
MPP

a, Capella
0.8 Towards

(ΔZ1~Z2)
75°06′

0.828

N ←

LOP
Regulus

Fix
(F)

Figure 11

130

distance between the two azimuths is determined; using the sine of this angle and the length of the second intercept, by the law of sines, sine 90° will establish the distance from the MPP to the fix. The direction to the fix is at right angles to the first azimuth. By mid-latitude sailing, the difference in latitude between the MPP and the fix is found to determine the latitude of the fix, and the departure is found and converted to the difference of longitude to permit establishing the longitude of the fix.

Example: Our EP is L 25° 03.′0 S, λ 119° 27.′5 W, when we observe Regulus to have a corrected sextant altitude, Ho, of 21° 30.′7, and Capella having a corrected altitude of 17° 59.′4. The coordinates of the fix resulting from these two observations are required, without plotting on a chart.

Figure 11 assists in visualizing what we are doing in calculating the position of the fix. It shows the two intercepts, the two lines of position, and the resulting fix, as well as the auxiliary right triangle, MXF, we used to determine the position of the fix.

We first reduce the Regulus observation, and obtain a computed altitude, Hc, of 21° 31.′9, and a Zn of 065° 12′. We now determine the MPP based on this sight by plane sailing

Ho	21° 30.′7	
Hc	21° 31.′9	
Intercept, *a*	1.′2 Away	Zn 065° 12′ (065.°2)

Since the intercept is Away, it will be 1.2 miles in the direction 245.°2, or S 65.°2 W from the EP. Using the law of sines, we find the departure, *p*, to be 1.09 miles West and the difference of latitude, *l*, to be 0.′503 S

$$90° : 1.2 :: 65° 12′ : 1.09, \quad \text{and} \quad 90° : 1.2 :: 24° 48′ : 0.′503$$

Using 25° 01.′8 as the mid-latitude, the *p* of 1.09 miles W is converted to 1.′2 W of longitude, DLo. We can now determine the coordinates of the MPP

EP	L 25° 03.′0 S	λ 119° 27.′5 W
l	0.′5 S	*DLo*	01.′2 W
MPP	L 25° 03.′5 S	λ 119° 28.′7 W

With this MPP, we reduce the Capella observation, obtaining an Hc of 17° 58.′6, and a Zn of 350° 06′. This yields an intercept of

Ho	17° 59.′4	
Hc	17° 58.′6	
Intercept, *a*	0.′8 Towards	Zn 350° 06′ (350.°1)

We next determine the angular distance between the two azimuths to be $75°06'$, $(360° - 350°06' = 9°54'; 9°54' + 65°12' = 75°06')$. Using the law of sines and the angle $75°06'$ found above, we now determine that the distance from the MPP to the fix is 0.828 miles

$$75°06' : 0.'8 :: 90° : 0.'828$$

The general direction of the fix, which lies at the intersection of the two lines of position, is determined by the azimuth and intercept of the second observation, $350°06.'0$ and 0.8 miles, respectively. As the intercept was *Towards,* it lies 0.828 miles, D in the formula below, in a roughly northerly direction from the MPP, at right angles to the azimuth of the first observation, which is $065°12'$; the actual direction, C in the formula, therefore is $335°12'$ $(065°12' + 270°)$. With this direction as a course, and the distance 0.828 miles, using the plane-sailing formulae, we can find, first, the difference of latitude between the MPP and the fix; then, first the departure, and then the difference of longitude between the two. *See* the right triangle, FMX, in Figure 11.

To find the difference of latitude, l, we use the formula

$$l = D \cos C$$

which we write

$$l = 0.828 \times \cos N \ 24°48' W$$

the course being $360° - 335°12'$.

Therefore, l is $0.'752$ N, or $0.'8$ N, which we subtract from the latitude of the MPP, $25°03.'5$ S, and obtain the latitude of the fix, $25°02.'7$ S.

The departure, p, we find by the formula

$$p = D \sin C$$

which here becomes

$$p = 0.828 \times \sin N \ 24°48' W = 0.347 \text{ miles W}$$

We next convert the departure to difference of longitude, DLo, using the formula

$$DLo = \frac{p}{\cos \text{ mid latitude}}$$

or

$$DLo = \frac{0.347}{\cos 25°03.'1} = 0.'383 \text{ W} (0.'4 \text{ W})$$

The longitude of the fix, therefore, is $119°29.'1$ W $(119°28.'7 + 0.'4)$.

Long-Term Sun Almanac

This *Long-Term Sun Almanac* permits the navigator to obtain the Greenwich hour angle, GHA, and declination, *d*, of the Sun with sufficient accuracy for the ordinary practice of marine navigation.

The *Almanac* is based on "Orbit Time," OT, which is time obtained by taking the Greenwich date and Greenwich mean time, GMT, of the observation *to the nearest hour,* and applying to it the correction found in Table A. Note that for leap years there are two corrections, the upper one being used for January and February, and the lower one for the balance of the year.

Thus, GMT 22-43-57, 16 March 1973, expressed to the nearest hour, would be 23 hours, 16 March 1973. Table A is now entered with the year 1973, and the correction (+) 6 hours is found. This would make the Orbit Time and date 05 hours, 17 March 1973 (23 hours on the 16th (+) 6 hours).

Next, Table B is entered with the Orbit date, and four quantities are extracted for zero hours of that date, these are (1) the value *E*; (2) the daily change in *E*, obtained by inspection, labeled plus or minus, according to whether *E* is increasing or decreasing numerically; (3) the declination; and (4) the tabulated daily rate of change in the declination. This last value is also given a sign, according to whether the declination is increasing or decreasing. *E*, incidentally, is the value of the Equation of Time, expressed in arc, plus 5°.

Table C is an interpolation table, whose entering arguments are hours of Orbit Time, and the daily changes in *E* and declination, found above. The values taken from Table C are applied to *E* and to the declination, according to their signs.

Tables D and E are tables of increments for hours, minutes, and seconds of *GMT* (*not* of Orbit Time); they are added to the value *E*, found above. Table D is a critical table; when the number of seconds of GMT coincide

133

with a tabulated value, take the increment to the right and directly above the tabulated value of time. Thus, for 03 minutes 57 seconds, the increment is $0° 59.'0$.

Table F gives the semidiameter, SD, of the Sun, the entering argument being the Greenwich date. The SD, as found in the table, should be applied to the altitude of the Sun as read from the sextant, the sign being ($+$) if the lower limb is observed, and ($-$) if the upper limb is observed.

The correction for the Sun's parallax is ($+$) $0.'1$ to altitude 65°. This should also be applied to the sextant altitude, together with the corrections for dip and refraction, described previously.

Example: Using the *Long-Term Sun Almanac,* we require the GHA and declination of the Sun for GMT 00-27-13, 7 December 1999.

The GMT, expressed to the nearest hour, is therefore 00 hours, 7 December 1999. Applying the correction for the year of 1999, of ($-$) 1 hour, obtained from Table A, we obtain Orbit Time 23 hours, 6 December. This we enter as shown in the form below.

The values of E and declination, obtained for 00 h of Orbit Time for the Orbit date, together with their daily changes, and the increments obtained from Tables C, D, and E are next entered in the form, and applied to the value of E and the tabulated declination to obtain the GHA and the corrected declination.

	GMT	00-27-13, 7 December 1999 to nearest hour is
		00 hours
Table A corr. time (1999)	($-$) 1 hour	
Orbit Time		23 hours, 6 December

Table B for 00 hours
Orbit time, 6 December E $7° 19'$, diff. ($-$) $7'$, d S $22° 25'$, diff. S $7'$

Table C for 23 hours
Orbit Time   ($-$) $7'$ S $7'$
                                          E $7° 12'$ S $22° 32'$

Table D 00 h 20 m GMT   ($+$) $180° 00'$

Table E   7 m 13 s GMT ($+$) $1° 48'$
                                    GHA $189° 00'$

When the problem is solved by use of the *Long-Term Sun Almanac,* therefore, at GMT 00-27-13, 7 December 1999, the GHA of the Sun is $189° 00'$, and the declination is S $22° 32'$.

A. Correction to GMT

Year	Corr.	Year	Corr.	Year	Corr.
	h		h		h
1965	+ 4	1977	+ 7	1989	+ 9
1966	− 1	1978	+ 1	1990	+ 3
1967	− 7	1979	− 5	1991	− 3
1968	−13	1980	−11	1992	− 9
1968	+11*	1980	+13*	1992	+15*
1969	+ 5	1981	+ 7	1993	+10
1970	− 1	1982	+ 1	1994	+ 4
1971	− 7	1983	− 4	1995	− 2
1972	−12	1984	−10	1996	− 8
1972	+12*	1984	+14*	1996	+16*
1973	+ 6	1985	+ 8	1997	+10
1974	0	1986	+ 2	1998	+ 4
1975	− 6	1987	− 4	1999	− 1
1976	−12	1988	− 9	2000	− 7
1976	+12*	1988	+15*	2000	+17*

* Correction to be used after 29 February.

B. Ephemeris of the Sun, Argument "Orbit Time"

OT 00ʰ	JANUARY E	d	Δ	FEBRUARY E	d	Δ	MARCH E	d	Δ
Date	° ′	° ′		° ′	° ′		° ′	° ′	
1	4 11	S.23 03	5	1 37	S.17 16	17	1 52	S. 7 49	23
2	4 04	22 58	5	1 35	16 59	17	1 55	7 26	23
3	3 57	22 53	6	1 33	16 42	18	1 58	7 03	23
4	3 50	22 47	6	1 31	16 24	18	2 01	6 40	23
5	3 43	22 41	7	1 30	16 06	18	2 04	6 17	23
6	3 36	S.22 34	7	1 29	S.15 48	18	2 07	S. 5 54	23
7	3 30	22 27	8	1 28	15 30	19	2 11	5 31	24
8	3 23	22 19	8	1 27	15 11	19	2 14	5 07	23
9	3 17	22 11	8	1 26	14 52	19	2 18	4 44	24
10	3 11	22 03	9	1 26	14 33	20	2 22	4 20	23
11	3 05	S.21 54	10	1 26	S.14 13	20	2 26	S. 3 57	24
12	2 59	21 44	9	1 26	13 53	20	2 30	3 33	23
13	2 53	21 35	10	1 26	13 33	20	2 34	3 10	24
14	2 47	21 25	11	1 26	13 13	20	2 38	2 46	24
15	2 42	21 14	11	1 27	12 53	21	2 42	2 22	23
16	2 37	S.21 03	11	1 27	S.12 32	20	2 46	S. 1 59	24
17	2 31	20 52	12	1 28	12 12	21	2 50	1 35	24
18	2 26	20 40	12	1 29	11 51	22	2 55	1 11	23
19	2 22	20 28	13	1 30	11 29	21	2 59	0 48	24
20	2 17	20 15	13	1 32	11 08	22	3 04	S. 0 24	24
21	2 13	S.20 02	13	1 33	S.10 46	21	3 08	0 00	24
22	2 08	19 49	14	1 35	10 25	22	3 12	N. 0 24	23
23	2 04	19 35	14	1 37	10 03	22	3 17	0 47	24
24	2 00	19 21	14	1 39	9 41	22	3 22	1 11	24
25	1 57	19 07	15	1 41	9 19	23	3 26	1 35	23
26	1 53	S.18 52	15	1 44	S. 8 56	22	3 31	N. 1 58	24
27	1 50	18 37	16	1 46	8 34	23	3 35	2 22	23
28	1 47	18 21	16	1 49	8 11	22	3 40	2 45	24
29	1 44	18 05	16	1 52	7 49	23	3 44	3 09	23
30	1 41	17 49	16				3 49	3 32	23
31	1 39	S.17 33	17				3 53	N. 3 55	23

B. Ephemeris of the Sun, Argument "Orbit Time" —*Continued*

OT 00ʰ Date	APRIL E	APRIL d		MAY E	MAY d		JUNE E	JUNE d	
	° ′	° ′		° ′	° ′		° ′	° ′	
1	3 58	N. 4 18	24	5 42	N.14 54	18	5 36	N.21 58	8
2	4 02	4 42	23	5 44	15 12	18	5 33	22 06	8
3	4 07	5 05	23	5 46	15 30	17	5 31	22 14	8
4	4 11	5 28	23	5 48	15 47	18	5 28	22 22	7
5	4 16	5 51	22	5 49	16 05	17	5 26	22 29	6
6	4 20	N. 6 13	23	5 50	N.16 22	17	5 23	N.22 35	7
7	4 24	6 36	23	5 51	16 39	16	5 21	22 42	5
8	4 28	6 59	22	5 52	16 55	17	5 18	22 47	6
9	4 33	7 21	22	5 53	17 12	16	5 15	22 53	5
10	4 37	7 43	23	5 54	17 28	15	5 12	22 58	5
11	4 41	N. 8 06	22	5 55	N.17 43	16	5 09	N.23 03	4
12	4 45	8 28	22	5 55	17 59	15	5 06	23 07	4
13	4 49	8 50	21	5 56	18 14	15	5 03	23 11	3
14	4 53	9 11	22	5 56	18 29	14	5 00	23 14	3
15	4 56	9 33	21	5 56	18 43	15	4 57	23 17	3
16	5 00	N. 9 54	22	5 56	N.18 58	13	4 54	N.23 20	2
17	5 04	10 16	21	5 55	19 11	14	4 50	23 22	2
18	5 07	10 37	21	5 55	19 25	13	4 47	23 24	1
19	5 10	10 58	21	5 54	19 38	13	4 44	23 25	1
20	5 14	11 19	20	5 54	19 51	13	4 41	23 26	0
21	5 17	N.11 39	21	5 53	N.20 04	12	4 37	N.23 26	1
22	5 20	12 00	20	5 52	20 16	12	4 34	23 27	1
23	5 23	12 20	20	5 51	20 28	11	4 31	23 26	1
24	5 26	12 40	20	5 50	20 39	11	4 28	23 25	1
25	5 29	13 00	19	5 48	20 50	11	4 24	23 24	1
26	5 31	N.13 19	19	5 47	N.21 01	11	4 21	N.23 23	2
27	5 34	13 38	20	5 45	21 12	10	4 18	23 21	2
28	5 36	13 58	19	5 44	21 22	9	4 15	23 19	3
29	5 38	14 17	18	5 42	21 31	10	4 12	23 16	3
30	5 40	14 35	19	5 40	21 41	9	4 09	23 13	4
31				5 38	N.21 50	8			

B. Ephemeris of the Sun, Argument "Orbit Time"—*Continued*

OT 00ʰ	JULY				AUGUST				SEPTEMBER			
	E ° ′	d ° ′			E ° ′	d ° ′			E ° ′	d ° ′		
Date												
1	4 06	N.23 09			3 25	N.18 10			4 57	N. 8 30		
2	4 03	23 05	4		3 26	17 55	15		5 01	8 08	22	
3	4 00	23 01	4		3 27	17 40	15		5 06	7 47	21	
4	3 57	22 56	5		3 28	17 24	16		5 11	7 25	22	
5	3 55	22 51	5		3 30	17 08	16		5 16	7 02	23	
6	3 52	N.22 45	6		3 31	N.16 52	16		5 21	N. 6 40	22	
7	3 49	22 39	6		3 33	16 36	16		5 26	6 18	22	
8	3 47	22 33	6		3 35	16 19	17		5 31	5 55	23	
9	3 45	22 26	7		3 37	16 02	17		5 36	5 33	22	
10	3 42	22 19	7		3 39	15 45	17		5 41	5 10	23	
11	3 40	N.22 11	8		3 41	N.15 27	18		5 47	N. 4 47	23	
12	3 38	22 03	8		3 43	15 09	18		5 52	4 25	22	
13	3 36	21 55	8		3 46	14 51	18		5 57	4 02	23	
14	3 35	21 46	9		3 48	14 33	18		6 02	3 39	23	
15	3 33	21 37	9		3 51	14 15	18		6 08	3 16	23	
16	3 31	N.21 28	9		3 54	N.13 56	19		6 13	N. 2 53	23	
17	3 30	21 18	10		3 57	13 37	19		6 18	2 30	23	
18	3 29	21 08	10		4 00	13 18	19		6 24	2 06	23	
19	3 28	20 58	10		4 04	12 59	19		6 29	1 43	24	
20	3 27	20 47	11		4 07	12 39	20		6 34	1 20	23	
21	3 26	N.20 36	11		4 11	N.12 19	20		6 40	N. 0 57	23	
22	3 25	20 24	12		4 14	11 59	20		6 45	0 33	24	
23	3 24	20 12	12		4 18	11 39	20		6 50	N. 0 10	23	
24	3 24	20 00	12		4 22	11 19	20		6 56	S. 0 13	23	
25	3 24	19 47	13		4 26	10 58	21		7 01	0 37	24	
26	3 23	N.19 34	13		4 30	N.10 38	20		7 06	S. 1 00	23	
27	3 23	19 21	13		4 34	10 17	21		7 11	1 24	24	
28	3 23	19 08	13		4 38	9 56	21		7 16	1 47	23	
29	3 24	18 54	14		4 43	9 35	21		7 21	2 10	23	
30	3 24	18 40	14		4 47	9 13	22		7 26	2 34	24	
31	3 25	N.18 25	15		4 52	N. 8 52	21					23
			15				22					

B. Ephemeris of the Sun, Argument "Orbit Time" —*Continued*

OT 00ʰ Date	OCTOBER E (° ')	OCTOBER d (° ')		NOVEMBER E (° ')	NOVEMBER d (° ')		DECEMBER d (° ')	
1	7 31	S. 2 57		9 05	S.14 14		7 48 S.21 42	
			23			19		10
2	7 36	3 20		9 06	14 33		7 43 21 52	
			24			19		9
3	7 41	3 44		9 06	14 52		7 37 22 01	
			23			19		8
4	7 45	4 07		9 06	15 11		7 31 22 09	
			23			19		8
5	7 50	4 30		9 06	15 30		7 25 22 17	
			23			18		8
6	7 55	S. 4 53		9 05	S.15 48		7 19 S.22 25	
			23			18		7
7	7 59	5 16		9 05	16 06		7 12 22 32	
			23			18		7
8	8 03	5 39		9 04	16 24		7 06 22 39	
			23			17		7
9	8 07	6 02		9 03	16 41		7 00 22 46	
			23			17		5
10	8 12	6 25		9 02	16 58		6 53 22 51	
			22			17		6
11	8 16	S. 6 47		9 00	S.17 15		6 46 S.22 57	
			23			17		5
12	8 19	7 10		8 59	17 32		6 39 23 02	
			23			16		4
13	8 23	7 33		8 57	17 48		6 32 23 06	
			22			16		5
14	8 27	7 55		8 55	18 04		6 25 23 11	
			22			16		3
15	8 30	8 17		8 52	18 20		6 18 23 14	
			23			15		3
16	8 34	S. 8 40		8 50	S.18 35		6 11 S.23 17	
			22			15		3
17	8 37	9 02		8 47	18 50		6 03 23 20	
			22			15		2
18	8 40	9 24		8 44	19 05		5 56 23 22	
			22			14		2
19	8 43	9 46		8 41	19 19		5 49 23 24	
			21			14		1
20	8 46	10 07		8 38	19 33		5 41 23 25	
			22			14		1
21	8 48	S.10 29		8 34	S.19 47		5 34 S.23 26	
			21			13		1
22	8 51	10 50		8 30	20 00		5 26 23 27	
			21			13		1
23	8 53	11 11		8 26	20 13		5 19 23 26	
			22			13		0
24	8 55	11 33		8 22	20 26		5 11 23 26	
			20			12		1
25	8 57	11 53		8 18	20 38		5 04 23 25	
			21			11		2
26	8 59	S.12 14		8 14	S.20 49		4 57 S.23 23	
			21			12		2
27	9 00	12 35		8 09	21 01		4 49 23 21	
			20			11		2
28	9 02	12 55		8 04	21 12		4 42 23 19	
			20			11		3
29	9 03	13 15		7 59	21 23		4 34 23 16	
			20			10		4
30	9 04	13 35		7 54	21 33		4 27 23 12	
			20			9		4
31	9 05	S.13 55					4 20 S.23 08	
			19					4

C. Interpolation of the Ephemeris for Hours of OT

Diff.	1 2 3	4 5 6	7 8 9	10 11 12	13 14 15	16 17 18	19 20 21	22 23 24
h	′ ′ ′	′ ′ ′	′ ′ ′	′ ′ ′	′ ′ ′	′ ′ ′	′ ′ ′	′ ′ ′
0	0 0 0	0 0 0	0 0 0	0 0 0	0 0 0	0 0 0	0 0 0	0 0 0
1	0 0 0	0 0 0	0 0 0	0 0 1	1 1 1	1 1 1	1 1 1	1 1 1
2	0 0 0	0 0 1	1 1 1	1 1 1	1 1 1	1 1 2	2 2 2	2 2 2
3	0 0 0	1 1 1	1 1 1	1 1 2	2 2 2	2 2 2	2 3 3	3 3 3
4	0 0 1	1 1 1	1 1 2	2 2 2	2 2 3	3 3 3	3 3 4	4 4 4
5	0 0 1	1 1 1	1 2 2	2 2 3	3 3 3	3 4 4	4 4 4	5 5 5
6	0 1 1	1 1 2	2 2 2	3 3 3	3 4 4	4 4 5	5 5 5	6 6 6
7	0 1 1	1 1 2	2 2 3	3 3 4	4 4 4	5 5 5	6 6 6	6 7 7
8	0 1 1	1 2 2	2 3 3	3 4 4	4 5 5	5 6 6	6 7 7	7 8 8
9	0 1 1	2 2 2	3 3 3	4 4 5	5 5 6	6 6 7	7 8 8	8 9 9
10	0 1 1	2 2 3	3 3 4	4 5 5	5 6 6	7 7 8	8 8 9	9 10 10
11	0 1 1	2 2 3	3 4 4	5 5 6	6 6 7	7 8 8	9 9 10	10 11 11
12	1 1 2	2 3 3	4 4 5	5 6 6	7 7 8	8 9 9	10 10 11	11 12 12
13	1 1 2	2 3 3	4 4 5	5 6 7	7 8 8	9 9 10	10 11 11	12 12 13
14	1 1 2	2 3 4	4 5 5	6 6 7	8 8 9	9 10 11	11 12 12	13 13 14
15	1 1 2	3 3 4	4 5 6	6 7 8	8 9 9	10 11 11	12 13 13	14 14 15
16	1 1 2	3 3 4	5 5 6	7 7 8	9 9 10	11 11 12	13 13 14	15 15 16
17	1 1 2	3 4 4	5 6 6	7 8 9	9 10 11	11 12 13	13 14 15	16 16 17
18	1 2 2	3 4 5	5 6 7	8 8 9	10 11 11	12 13 14	14 15 16	17 17 18
19	1 2 2	3 4 5	6 6 7	8 9 10	10 11 12	13 13 14	15 16 17	17 18 19
20	1 2 3	3 4 5	6 7 8	8 9 10	11 12 13	13 14 15	16 17 18	18 19 20
21	1 2 3	4 4 5	6 7 8	9 10 11	11 12 13	14 15 16	17 18 18	19 20 21
22	1 2 3	4 5 6	6 7 8	9 10 11	12 13 14	15 16 17	17 18 19	20 21 22
23	1 2 3	4 5 6	7 8 9	10 11 12	12 13 14	15 16 17	18 19 20	21 22 23

D. Increment of GHA Sun: Hours and Tens of Minutes of GMT

h	00^m	10^m	20^m	30^m	40^m	50^m
	° ′	° ′	° ′	° ′	° ′	° ′
00	175 00	177 30	180 00	182 30	185 00	187 30
01	190 00	192 30	195 00	197 30	200 00	202 30
02	205 00	207 30	210 00	212 30	215 00	217 30
03	220 00	222 30	225 00	227 30	230 00	232 30
04	235 00	237 30	240 00	242 30	245 00	247 30
05	250 00	252 30	255 00	257 30	260 00	262 30
06	265 00	267 30	270 00	272 30	275 00	277 30
07	280 00	282 30	285 00	287 30	290 00	292 30
08	295 00	297 30	300 00	302 30	305 00	307 30
09	310 00	312 30	315 00	317 30	320 00	322 30
10	325 00	327 30	330 00	332 30	335 00	337 30
11	340 00	342 30	345 00	347 30	350 00	352 30
12	355 00	357 30	0 00	2 30	5 00	7 30
13	10 00	12 30	15 00	17 30	20 00	22 30
14	25 00	27 30	30 00	32 30	35 00	37 30
15	40 00	42 30	45 00	47 30	50 00	52 30
16	55 00	57 30	60 00	62 30	65 00	67 30
17	70 00	72 30	75 00	77 30	80 00	82 30
18	85 00	87 30	90 00	92 30	95 00	97 30
19	100 00	102 30	105 00	107 30	110 00	112 30
20	115 00	117 30	120 00	122 30	125 00	127 30
21	130 00	132 30	135 00	137 30	140 00	142 30
22	145 00	147 30	150 00	152 30	155 00	157 30
23	160 00	162 30	165 00	167 30	170 00	172 30

Reproduced by permission of H.M. Nautical Almanac Office, Royal Greenwich Observatory.

E. Increment of GHA Sun: Minutes and Seconds of GMT

m s	° ′	m s	° ′	m s	° ′	m s	° ′	m s	° ′	m s	° ′
00 00	0 00	01 37	0 25	03 17	0 50	04 57	1 15	06 37	1 40	08 17	2 05
01	0 01	41	0 26	21	0 51	05 01	1 16	41	1 41	21	2 06
05	0 02	45	0 27	25	0 52	05	1 17	45	1 42	25	2 07
09	0 03	49	0 28	29	0 53	09	1 18	49	1 43	29	2 08
13	0 04	53	0 29	33	0 54	13	1 19	53	1 44	33	2 09
17	0 05	01 57	0 30	37	0 55	17	1 20	06 57	1 45	37	2 10
21	0 06	02 01	0 31	41	0 56	21	1 21	07 01	1 46	41	2 11
25	0 07	05	0 32	45	0 57	25	1 22	05	1 47	45	2 12
29	0 08	09	0 33	49	0 57	29	1 22	09	1 47	49	2 12
33	0 08	13	0 33	53	0 58	33	1 23	13	1 48	53	2 13
37	0 09	17	0 34	03 57	0 59	37	1 24	17	1 49	08 57	2 14
41	0 10	21	0 35	04 01	1 00	41	1 25	21	1 50	09 01	2 15
45	0 11	25	0 36	05	1 01	45	1 26	25	1 51	05	2 16
49	0 12	29	0 37	09	1 02	49	1 27	29	1 52	09	2 17
53	0 13	33	0 38	13	1 03	53	1 28	33	1 53	13	2 18
00 57	0 14	37	0 39	17	1 04	05 57	1 29	37	1 54	17	2 19
01 01	0 15	41	0 40	21	1 05	06 01	1 30	41	1 55	21	2 20
05	0 16	45	0 41	25	1 06	05	1 31	45	1 56	25	2 21
09	0 17	49	0 42	29	1 07	09	1 32	49	1 57	29	2 22
13	0 18	53	0 43	33	1 08	13	1 33	53	1 58	33	2 23
17	0 19	02 57	0 44	37	1 09	17	1 34	07 57	1 59	37	2 24
21	0 20	03 01	0 45	41	1 10	21	1 35	08 01	2 00	41	2 25
25	0 21	05	0 46	45	1 11	25	1 36	05	2 01	45	2 26
29	0 22	09	0 47	49	1 12	29	1 37	09	2 02	49	2 27
33	0 23	13	0 48	53	1 13	33	1 38	13	2 03	53	2 28
37	0 24	17	0 49	04 57	1 14	37	1 39	17	2 04	09 57	2 29
01 41	0 25	03 21	0 50	05 01	1 15	06 41	1 40	08 21	2 05	10 00	2 30

F. Sun's Semidiameter

Date			SD
1 January	—	2 February	16.'3
3 February	—	4 March	16.'2
5 March	—	28 March	16.'1
29 March	—	18 April	16.'0
19 April	—	15 May	15.'9
16 May	—	25 August	15.'8
26 August	—	18 September	15.'9
19 September	—	12 October	16.'0
13 October	—	2 November	16.'1
3 November	—	2 December	16.'2
3 December	—	31 December	16.'3

The correction for parallax in Sun observations is (+) 0.'1 to altitude 65°.

Long-Term Star Almanac

With the *Long-Term Star Almanac,* the Greenwich hour angle, GHA, and declination of 38 major stars may be obtained. The maximum error arising in a star altitude computed by means of this almanac should not exceed 1.3 minutes of arc.

Table A of this almanac serves to provide the Greenwich hour angle, GHA, of Aries for the time of the observation; Table B furnishes the sidereal hour angle, SHA, and declination of the star; Table C is a multiplication table; and Table D gives decimal parts of a year.

To obtain the GHA of Aries, we subtract 1956 from the current year, then divide the difference by 4, thus obtaining (a) a whole number, and (b) a remainder, which will be 0, 1, 2, or 3.

In entering Table A, we use two arguments: *the remainder* found above and *the current or required month.* From the column headed with the same numeral as the remainder, we extract the angular value shown for the month required, and note it in a form similar to the one used in the following example.

Next we enter Table C and, using the whole number found in step (a) above as argument, extract from Column 1 the tabulated value and enter it in the form. With the day of the month as argument, we take the tabulated value from Column 2 and note it in the form. Similarly, with the whole hour of GMT as argument, we enter Column 3 and note the tabulated value in the form. We next enter Column 4, with the minutes of GMT as argument, extract the tabulated value, and note that in the form. Finally, we enter Column 5, our argument being the seconds of GMT, and extract and note the tabulated value.

The sum of our listed values represents the GHA Aries at the time of the observation.

We now turn to Table B and, for the desired star, take out and note the base SHA for 1 January 1956, the declination, and the annual corrections for each. Next, using Table D, we convert the current day and month to a decimal of a year, and apply it to the current year, thus 26 May 1971 would become 1970.4. From this, we subtract 1956.0, then multiply the difference by the annual corrections for SHA and declination. These are then applied, according to their signs, to the SHA and declination of the star for 1956.0, which we have already entered in the form. Note particularly that the correction to the declination is applied with its sign as stated, regardless of the name of the declination. Thus, if the declination is named South, and the sign of the correction is $(+)$, the corrected declination will be greater in value than the tabulated.

We now have the SHA and declination, corrected for the date. The SHA added to the GHA of Aries, previously determined, yields the GHA of the star. The sight can now be worked in the usual manner.

Example: Using the *Long-Term Star Almanac,* we need to find GHA Aries, SHA Sirius, GHA Sirius, and declination of Sirius for GMT 17-14-47, 23 November 1970.

We subtract 1956 from 1970; the difference is 14, which we divide by 4, giving us, first, the whole number, 3, then the remainder, 2. Using the remainder as argument, we now enter the column headed "2" in Table A and opposite the current month, November, we find the value 38°47.'4. This we note in the form. Using the whole number, 3, as the argument, we enter Column 1 in Table C, and note the appropriate value, 5.'5. We next extract the value for 23 days, 22°40.'2, from Column 2, the value for 17 hours from Column 3, that for 14 minutes from Column 4, and that for 47 seconds from Column 5. Each is entered in the form, as shown, and their sum is the GHA Aries; 360° being subtracted, should the sum exceed that figure.

Table	Column	Argument	D	M
A		"2" and November	38	47.4
C	1	"3"		5.5
C	2	23 days	22	40.2
C	3	17 hours	255	41.9
C	4	14 minutes	3	30.6
C	5	47 seconds		11.8
		GHA Aries =	320	57.4

Determination of GHA Aries is a lengthy process. When several stars are to be observed within the same whole hour of GMT, use of a subtotal simplifies this determination. The subtotal would be the sum of the first four entries. For additional star sights, only the arguments for increments of minutes and seconds for each sight would be added to the subtotal to obtain each GHA Aries.

We will now proceed to obtain the SHA Sirius and the declination of Sirius.

Entering Table B, we extract the tabulated values of SHA and declination of Sirius, together with their respective correction factors and their signs, and enter them in the form shown below. To obtain the multiplier for these correction factors, we use Table D, and find that 23 November 1970 is expressed as 1970.9. The difference between 1970.9 and 1956.0 is 14.9. Therefore, 14.9 is the multiplier for the correction factors.

Table B

	D	M	
SHA Sirius, 1956.0	259	11.9	Corr. factor $(-)\,0.'66$
$(-)$		9.8	$14.9 \times (-)\,0.'66$
SHA Sirius, 1970.9 $=$	259	2.1	

	D	M	
Declination of Sirius, 1956.0	S 16	39.3	Corr. factor $(+)\,0.'08$
$(+)$		1.2	$14.9 \times (+)\,0.'08$
Declination of Sirius, 1970.9 $=$	S 16	40.5	

All that remains is to add GHA Aries to SHA Sirius to obtain GHA Sirius for the time and date required:

	D	M
GHA Aries	320	57.4
SHA Sirius	259	02.1
	579	59.5
$(-)\,360$		
GHA Sirius	219	59.5

Therefore,

		D	M
GHA Aries is		320	57.4
SHA Sirius is		259	02.1
GHA Sirius is		219	59.5
Declination of Sirius is	S	16	40.5

By the *Nautical Almanac*

GHA Aries is	320° 57.'4
SHA Sirius is	259° 01.'7
Declination of Sirius is	S 16° 40.'3

Form for use with Long-Term Star Almanac

Date 23 NOV. 70	GMT 17-14-47	Star SIRIUS

$(1956.0) \sim \dfrac{\text{Current Year}}{\text{and Decimal}} = \dfrac{\text{Difference}}{4} = \begin{array}{l}\text{(a) whole number and,}\\ \text{(b) remainder}\end{array}$

TABLE	COLUMN	ARGUMENT	° ′	° ′
A	—	(b) and month "2"½ NOV. 38 47.4		
C	1	(a) "3" 5.5		
C	2	Days 23 22 40.2		
C	3	Hours 17 255 41.9		
		Subtotal	317 15.0	
C	4	Minutes 14 3 30.6		
C	5	Seconds 47 11.8		
		Subtotal	3 42.4	
		GHA Aries	320 57.4	
B & D		SHA (1956.0) 259 11.9		
		Annual corr. factor (±) , (−) 0.66 × △ years and decimal of year 14.9 = (−) 9.8		
		SHA (1970.9) 259 02.1		
B & D		Declination corr. factor (±) (1956.0) N/S S 16 39.3		
		Annual corr. factor (±) , (+) 0.08 × △ years and decimal of year 14.9 = (+) 1.2		
		DECLINATION N/S S 16 40.5		

Having obtained the SHA and declination of the star for the date and time of the observation, the latter is reduced in the regular manner.

A. Aries (♈)

0		1		Month	2		3	
°	′	°	′		°	′	°	′
98	38.9	99	23.6	January	99	09.3	98	54.9
129	12.2	129	57.0	February	129	42.6	129	28.2
157	47.2	157	32.8	March	157	18.4	157	04.0
188	20.5	188	06.1	April	187	51.7	187	37.3
217	54.6	217	40.3	May	217	25.9	217	11.5
248	27.9	248	13.6	June	247	59.2	247	44.8
278	02.1	277	47.7	July	277	33.3	277	18.9
308	35.4	308	21.1	August	308	06.7	307	52.2
339	08.7	338	54.3	September	338	39.9	338	25.5
8	42.9	8	28.5	October	8	14.1	7	59.7
39	16.2	39	01.8	November	38	47.4	38	33.0
68	50.3	68	35.9	December	68	21.5	68	07.1

B. Stars

SHA (1956.0)		Annual Corr.	Star	Dec. (1956.0)		Annual Corr.
°	′	′		°	′	′
315	51.1	− 0.57	Acamar	40	28.8 S	− 0.24
335	58.8	− 0.56	Achernar	57	27.6 S	− 0.30
173	57.9	− 0.84	Acrux	62	51.3 S	+ 0.33
291	39.1	− 0.86	Aldebaran	16	25.3 N	+ 0.12
153	32.9	− 0.59	Alkaid	49	31.9 N	− 0.30
218	38.6	− 0.74	Alphard	8	28.0 S	+ 0.26
126	47.7	− 0.64	Alphecca	26	51.7 N	− 0.20
358	28.4	− 0.78	Alpheratz	28	50.9 N	+ 0.33
62	50.5	− 0.73	Altair	8	45.0 N	+ 0.16
113	19.4	− 0.92	Antares	26	20.2 S	+ 0.13
146	35.2	− 0.68	Arcturus	19	24.6 N	− 0.31
109	00.2	− 1.59	Atria	68	57.0 S	+ 0.11
271	48.2	− 0.81	Betelgeuse	7	24.0 N	+ 0.01
264	15.4	− 0.33	Canopus	52	40.3 S	+ 0.03
281	38.5	− 1.11	Capella	45	57.3 N	+ 0.06

B. Stars—*Continued*

SHA (1956.0)		Annual Corr.	Star	Dec. (1956.0)		Annual Corr.
°	′	′		°	′	′
50	01.0	−0.51	Deneb	45	07.3 N	+0.21
183	17.8	−0.76	Denebola	14	49.1 N	−0.34
349	39.3	−0.75	Diphda	18	13.7 S	−0.33
194	44.6	−0.92	Dubhe	61	59.3 N	−0.32
34	29.6	−0.74	Enif	9	40.3 N	+0.28
16	11.6	−0.83	Fomalhaut	29	51.4 S	−0.32
328	49.7	−0.85	Hamal	23	15.3 N	+0.28
137	17.8	+0.04	Kochab	74	20.1 N	−0.25
148	58.7	−0.88	Menkent	36	09.3 S	+0.29
309	42.5	−1.07	Mirfak	49	42.4 N	+0.21
76	51.9	−0.93	Nunki	26	21.2 S	−0.08
54	27.3	−1.19	Peacock	56	52.7 S	−0.19
244	20.6	−0.92	Pollux	28	08.0 N	−0.15
245	45.0	−0.78	Procyon	5	20.4 N	−0.15
96	46.6	−0.70	Rasalhague	12	35.4 N	−0.04
208	29.5	−0.80	Regulus	12	11.0 N	−0.29
281	53.7	−0.72	Rigel	8	15.1 S	−0.07
140	51.0	−1.02	Rigil Kent.	60	39.3 S	+0.25
350	30.1	−0.85	Schedar	56	17.8 N	+0.33
259	11.9	−0.66	Sirius	16	39.3 S	+0.08
159	16.9	−0.79	Spica	10	55.9 S	+0.31
223	24.4	−0.55	Suhail	43	15.2 S	+0.24
81	08.3	−0.51	Vega	38	44.5 N	+0.06

C. Multiplication Table

No.	1	2		3		4		5
	′	°	′	°	′	°	′	′
1	1.8	0	59.1	15	02.5	0	15.0	0.2
2	3.7	1	58.3	30	04.9	0	30.1	0.5
3	5.5	2	57.4	45	07.4	0	45.1	0.8
4	7.4	3	56.6	60	09.9	1	00.2	1.0
5	9.2	4	55.7	75	12.3	1	15.2	1.2
6	11.0	5	54.8	90	14.8	1	30.2	1.5
7	12.9	6	54.0	105	17.2	1	45.3	1.8
8	14.7	7	53.1	120	19.7	2	00.3	2.0
9	16.6	8	52.3	135	22.2	2	15.4	2.2
10	18.4	9	51.4	150	24.6	2	30.4	2.5
11	20.2	10	50.5	165	27.1	2	45.5	2.8
12	22.1	11	49.7	180	29.6	3	00.5	3.0
13	23.9	12	48.8	195	32.0	3	15.5	3.2
14	25.8	13	48.0	210	34.5	3	30.6	3.5
15	27.6	14	47.1	225	37.0	3	45.6	3.8
16	29.4	15	46.2	240	39.4	4	00.7	4.0
17	31.3	16	45.4	255	41.9	4	15.7	4.2
18	33.1	17	44.5	270	44.4	4	30.7	4.5
19	35.0	18	43.7	285	46.8	4	45.8	4.8
20	36.8	19	42.8	300	49.3	5	00.8	5.0
21	38.6	20	41.9	315	51.7	5	15.9	5.2
22	40.5	21	41.1	330	54.2	5	30.9	5.5
23	42.3	22	40.2	345	56.7	5	45.9	5.8
24	44.2	23	39.4	360	59.1	6	01.0	6.0
25	46.0	24	38.5	—		6	16.0	6.2
26	47.8	25	37.6	—		6	31.1	6.5
27	49.7	26	36.8	—		6	46.1	6.8
28	51.5	27	35.9	—		7	01.1	7.0
29	53.4	28	35.1	—		7	16.2	7.2
30	55.2	29	34.2	—		7	31.2	7.5
31	57.0	30	33.3	—		7	46.3	7.8
32	58.9	—		—		8	01.3	8.0
33	60.7	—		—		8	16.4	8.2
34	62.6	—		—		8	31.4	8.5
35	64.6	—		—		8	46.4	8.8

C. Multiplication Table—*Continued*

No.	1	2	3	4	5
	′	° ′	° ′	° ′	′
36	66.2	—	—	9 01.5	9.0
37	68.1	—	—	9 16.5	9.2
38	69.9	—	—	9 31.6	9.5
39	71.8	—	—	9 46.6	9.8
40	73.6	—	—	10 01.6	10.0
41	75.4	—	—	10 16.7	10.2
42	77.3	—	—	10 31.7	10.5
43	79.1	—	—	10 46.8	10.8
44	81.0	—	—	11 01.8	11.0
45	82.8	—	—	11 16.8	11.2
46	84.6	—	—	11 31.9	11.5
47	86.5	—	—	11 46.9	11.8
48	88.3	—	—	12 02.0	12.0
49	90.2	—	—	12 17.0	12.2
50	92.0	—	—	12 32.1	12.5
51	93.8	—	—	12 47.1	12.8
52	95.7	—	—	13 02.1	13.0
53	97.5	—	—	13 17.2	13.2
54	99.4	—	—	13 32.2	13.5
55	—	—	—	13 47.3	13.8
56	—	—	—	14 02.3	14.0
57	—	—	—	14 17.3	14.2
58	—	—	—	14 32.4	14.5
59	—	—	—	14 47.4	14.8
60	—	—	—	15 02.5	15.0

D. Decimal Parts of Year

Decimal	0.0	0.1	0.2	0.3	0.4	0.5	0.6	0.7	0.8	0.9	1.0
Day of Year	Jan. 1 to Jan. 18	Jan. 19 to Feb. 23	Feb. 24 to Apr. 1	Apr. 2 to May 7	May 8 to June 13	June 14 to July 19	July 20 to Aug. 25	Aug. 26 to Sept. 30	Oct. 1 to Nov. 6	Nov. 7 to Dec. 12	Dec. 13 to Dec. 31

U.S. Naval Oceanographic Office, H.O. Publication No. 9 (Bowditch).

Miscellaneous Computations

Temperature Conversion

Temperature expressed in degrees Fahrenheit may readily be converted to degrees Celsius (Centigrade), and vice versa, by means of the formulae given below, in which F stands for degrees Fahrenheit, and C for degrees Celsius.

To convert degrees F to degrees C, the formula is

$$C = \tfrac{5}{9}(F - 32°) \tag{1}$$

The conversion of degrees Celsius to degrees Fahrenheit is by the formula

$$F = \tfrac{9}{5}(C + 32°) \tag{2}$$

Example 1: We wish to convert 63° F to degrees C. We write Formula (1)

$$C = \tfrac{5}{9} \times (63° - 32°) = \tfrac{5}{9} \times 31° = 17.°2\,C$$

Example 2: We wish to convert $-23.°8\,C$ to degrees F. We write Formula (2)

$$F = (\tfrac{9}{5} \times -23.°8) + 32° = -42.°8 + 32° = -10.°8\,F$$

Example 3: We wish to convert 26° F to degrees C. Formula (1) becomes

$$C = \tfrac{5}{9} \times (26° - 32°) = \tfrac{5}{9} \times -6° = -3.°3\,C$$

Barometric-Pressure Conversion

Inches of mercury, millimeters of mercury, and millibars may be inter-converted with sufficient accuracy for all ordinary purposes by means of the slide rule and the following formulae.

To find the atmospheric pressure in inches of mercury, when it is stated in millibars, the formula is

$$IM = 0.02953 \times Mbs \tag{1}$$

where IM is pressure in inches of mercury, and Mbs represents the number of millibars.

To convert inches of mercury to millibars, the formula is

$$Mbs = \frac{IM}{0.02953} \tag{2}$$

When atmospheric pressure is stated in millimeters of mercury, the equivalent value in millibars may be found by the formula

$$Mbs = \frac{Mm}{0.75} \tag{3}$$

in which Mm represents the atmospheric pressure stated in millimeters.

Example 1: The atmospheric pressure is given as 998 millibars; we wish to convert this to read inches of mercury. Formula (1) becomes

$$IM = 0.02953 \times 998 = 29.47$$

The atmospheric pressure is, therefore, 29.47 inches.

Example 2: The barometer reads 30.56 inches; we wish to state it in millibars. We use Formula (2), which we write

$$Mbs = \frac{30.56}{0.02953} = 1035$$

Therefore, 1035 millibars are the equivalent of 30.56 inches of mercury.

Example 3: The atmospheric pressure is given as 764 millimeters of mercury, which we wish to convert to millibars. We write Formula (3)

$$Mbs = \frac{764}{0.75} = 1019$$

The pressure expressed in millibars is, therefore, 1019.

Fuel Consumption

For large ships steaming at economical speeds, that is, well below hull speed, *fuel consumption varies as the cube of the speed for a given time, and as the square of the speed for a given distance.*

For *time,* the formula is

$$\frac{S_2^3}{S_1^3} \times F_1 = F_2 \tag{1}$$

where S_1 is the speed for which the fuel consumption in known, S_2 is the speed for which the fuel consumption is desired, F_1 is the fuel in units consumed per hour or per day at S_1, and F_2 is fuel consumed at the new speed.

For *distance,* the formula is

$$\frac{S_2^2}{S_1^2} \times F_1 = F_2 \tag{2}$$

using the same notation as in Formula (1).

Example 1: At 14 knots we burn 40 tons of fuel a day. What will be our fuel consumption per day at 12 knots?

The cube of 14 is 2744, and the cube of 12 is 1728, so we write Formula (1)

$$\frac{S_2^3 \; 1728}{S_1^3 \; 2744} \times F_1 \; 40 = F_2 \; 25.2$$

Fuel consumption at 12 knots will, therefore, be 25.2 tons per day.

Example 2: At 13 knots we burn 2.65 tons of fuel per hour, and we wish to determine our hourly fuel consumption at 15 knots.

The cube of 13 is 2197, and the cube of 15 is 3375. We, therefore, write Formula (1)

$$\frac{S_2^3 \; 3375}{S_1^3 \; 2197} \times F_1 \; 2.65 = F_2 \; 4.07$$

At 15 knots our hourly fuel consumption will, therefore, be 4.07 tons.

Example 3: At 13 knots we require 323 tons of fuel to steam 2,085 miles. How much fuel will we require to steam the same distance at 15 knots?

In this case, we use Formula (2), which we write

$$\frac{S_2^2 \; 225}{S_1^2 \; 169} \times F_1 \; 323 = F_2 \; 430$$

We will, therefore, require 430 tons of fuel to cover 2,085 miles at 15 knots.

By rearranging or transposing factors as required, Formulae (1) and (2), above, can be used to solve variations of these fuel-consumption problems.

Example 4: We know that we require 323 tons of fuel to make a run of 2,085 miles at 13 knots. What speed must we use to make the same run using only 260 tons of fuel?

In this case, S_2 is not known, but F_2 is, so we transpose Formula (2) to read

$$S_2^2 = \frac{F_2 \times S_1^2}{F_1}$$

which becomes

$$S_2^2 = \frac{260 \times 169}{323} = 136$$

The square of the speed we must use to cover the required distance on 260 tons of fuel is 136.

Therefore, the required speed is the square root of 136, or 11.66 knots.

Example 5: We know that our ship burns 323 tons of fuel to travel 2,085 miles at 13 knots. We wish to determine how much fuel we would require to travel 1,850 miles at 16 knots.

We first determine how much fuel she would consume steaming the first distance, 2,085 miles, at 16 knots. Formula (2) becomes

$$\frac{S_2^2 \; 256}{S_1^2 \; 169} \times F_1 \; 323 = F_2 \; 490$$

For 2,085 miles at 16 knots, we would require 490 tons of fuel.

We can now find the amount of fuel required to steam 1,850 miles at 16 knots

$$D_1 \ 2,085 \text{ miles} : D_2 \ 1,850 \text{ miles} :: F_2 \ 490 \text{ tons} : F_3 \ 435 \text{ tons}$$

We would, therefore, require 435 tons to steam 1,850 miles at 16 knots.

Some fuel problems are best solved by ratios. The following example is a case in point.

Example 6: We know that our ship requires 323 tons of fuel to travel 2,085 miles at 13 knots. At what speed must we steam to travel 3,450 miles on 400 tons of fuel?

We first determine how many miles we would cover at 13 knots on 400 tons of fuel. For this purpose, we use the ratio

$$F_1 : F_2 :: D_1 : D_2$$

in which D_1 is the known distance and D_2 is the distance to be found, and we write

$$F_1 \ 323 : F_2 \ 400 :: D_1 \ 2,085 : D_2 \ 2,582$$

At 13 knots, therefore, we would cover 2,582 miles on 400 tons. Next, using the ratio

$$D_2 : D_3 :: F_2 : F_3$$

we find how many tons of fuel would be required to steam 3,450 miles at 13 knots

$$D_2 \ 2,582 : D_3 \ 3,450 :: F_2 \ 400 : F_3 \ 534$$

We would, therefore, require 534 tons of fuel for 3,450 miles at 13 knots. Now, using a third ratio

$$F_3 : F_2 :: S_1^2 : S_2^2$$

we can determine the speed required to traverse 3,450 miles on 400 tons of fuel

$$F_3 \ 534 : F_2 \ 400 :: S_1^2 \ 169 : S_2^2 \ 126.5$$

The square of the required speed is, therefore, 126.5, and its square root is 11.25.

Therefore, we must steam at 11.25 knots to cover 3,450 miles on 400 tons of fuel.

Propeller Slip

Apparent propeller slip is the difference between the pitch of a propeller multiplied by the number of revolutions it makes and the vessel's advance. Slip is expressed as a percentage. Thus, a steamer turning a propeller having a 20-foot pitch at 152 revolutions per minute (rpm) would move 3,040 feet in one minute, or would be steaming at almost exactly 30.0 knots (actually, 30.02)

$$\frac{3,040 \text{ feet} \times 60 \text{ minutes}}{6,076 \text{ feet}}$$

If she made 27.0 knots, the slip would be 10% (27 : 30 : : 90 : 100).

In working with the slide rule, the length of the nautical mile is generally considered to be 6,080 feet; in fact, its length is 6,076.11548556 feet.

Slip varies tremendously with vessel type. Under fine weather conditions, the slip for a large freighter driven at an economical speed by a slow-turning propeller may approach a highly favorable 5%. On the other hand, for a heavy auxiliary sailboat turning a small propeller at a high number of revolutions, it may approach 50% in smooth water, and on a windless day. Head winds and head seas, of course, greatly increase the slip, and high speeds have the same effect on many vessels.

For small craft of various types, average slip is approximately as listed below:

Fast open motor boats	± 20%
Light cruisers	± 25%
Heavy cruisers	± 28%
Auxiliary sailboats	± 33% to 50%

A graph or table showing the number of engine or propeller turns per minute required to achieve any given speed in still water is most helpful. For large cargo carriers, graphs or tables for various loadings are required.

The diameter and pitch of propellers for small craft are stamped on the wheel, and are usually given in inches.

To find the speed in knots a propeller would give a boat, if there were no slip, we could use the formula

$$\text{Speed in knots} = \frac{\text{propeller rpm} \times \text{pitch in inches} \times 60 \text{ minutes}}{6{,}080 \text{ feet} \times 12 \text{ inches}}$$

However, this formula can be more simply written

$$\text{Speed in knots} = \text{propeller rpm} \times \text{pitch in inches} \times 0.000822 \quad\quad (1)$$

because $\dfrac{60}{6{,}080 \times 12} = 0.000822$

To find speed in miles per hour, we would substitute 0.000947 as the constant $\dfrac{60}{5{,}280 \times 12} = 0.000947$

Example 1: Our propeller has a pitch of 22 inches. If there were no slip, what would be our speed in knots, if the propeller were turning at 1,800 rpm?

Here, we use Formula (1) and the constant 0.000822, and write

$$\text{Speed in knots} = 1{,}800 \times 22 \times 0.000822 = 32.55$$

In the absence of slip, we would, therefore, make 32.55 knots.

Now let us assume that when our propeller is turning at 1,800 rpm, we are actually making 22.5 knots, and we wish to determine the slip. We use the ratio

$$22.5 : 32.55 :: 69.1 : 100$$

The slip, therefore, is 30.9% (100 − 69.1). Remember that the slip percentage is based on the propeller pitch and its rpm and *not* on the speed made good.

For ships, propeller pitch is stated in feet and inches or feet and decimals of feet. If it is stated in feet and inches, the inches should be converted to decimals. Thus, for a pitch of 18 feet 3 inches, we would use 18.25 feet. To find the ship's speed if there were no slip, the formula would be

$$\text{Speed in knots} = \frac{\text{propeller rpm} \times \text{pitch in feet} \times 60 \text{ minutes}}{6{,}080}$$

However, this also can be simplified

$$\text{Speed in knots} = \text{propeller rpm} \times \text{pitch in feet} \times 0.00987 \quad\quad (2)$$

because 60 divided by 6076 gives the constant 0.00987.

Example 2: Our propeller pitch is 11 feet 6 inches, and we wish to know what speed we would obtain at 170 rpm, if there were no slip. We write Formula (2)

$$\text{Speed in knots} = 170 \times 11.5 \times 0.00987 = 19.3$$

Our speed, therefore, would be 19.3 knots.

Suppose that we wanted to allow for 11% slip, and still obtain a speed of 19.3 knots. How many shaft rpm should we call for?

We arrive at the required number of rpm by using the ratio

$$89\% : 170 \text{ rpm} :: 100\% : 191 \text{ rpm}$$

To make 19.3 knots we should, therefore, call for 191 rpm.

The engine rooms of large vessels have revolution counters, which record the number of turns the shaft has made in a given period. If the value of the slip is known, such counters are most useful in determining the distance run over a given period: all that is required is to calculate how far the ship would have advanced for the given pitch and number of turns, and apply the slip to the result of that calculation.

Example 3: Our propeller pitch is 11 feet 6 inches, and the shaft counters show that we have made 28,300 propeller revolutions in a given period. We wish to determine how far we have steamed, allowing for an 11% slip.

The slip being 11%, we multiply the advance by 0.89 $(1 - 0.11)$. We then have

$$\text{Miles steamed} = \frac{\text{pitch 11.5 feet} \times 28{,}300 \text{ shaft revolutions} \times 0.89 \text{ slip factor}}{6{,}080 \text{ feet}}$$

$$= 47.6$$

Allowing for an 11% slip, we have, therefore, steamed 47.6 miles.

Rigging Loads

The load on masts, booms, derricks, and shear legs, as well as on their rigging, can be determined by means of the slide rule considerably more rapidly and accurately than by construction. Essentially, the process involves solving the triangles in a parallelogram of forces by trigonometry rather than by construction and careful linear measurement.

Let us assume that a naval architect has specified that the headstay to the bowsprit on a sailboat must have a tensile strength of 12,000 lbs., which allows for a factor of safety of 4 to 1. We wish to determine what the tensile strength of the bobstay should be, allowing for the same safety factor, and what the compression load would be on the bowsprit at the stays' tensile limit.

We first determine that the angles made by the headstay and the bobstay with the bowsprit are 70° and 24°, respectively; *see* Figure 12-a. The resulting parallelogram of forces is shown in Figure 12-b, but we do not need to draw it. To help visualize the solution, which we obtain by the law of sines, we can sketch the triangle forming the upper half of the parallelogram; *see* Figure 12-c. In this triangle, the side *AB* represents the headstay; its length represents the tensile strength of the wire, 12,000 lbs. The length of the side *AC* will then represent the required tensile strength of the bobstay, and the length of *BC* the compression load on the bowsprit, when the headstay is loaded to 12,000 lbs. Now

$$\sin 24° \ (\lfloor C) : 12{,}000 \ \text{lbs} :: \sin 86° \ (\lfloor A) : 29{,}400 \ \text{lbs} \ (BC)$$
$$:: \sin 70° \ (\lfloor B) : 27{,}700 \ \text{lbs} \ (AC)$$

Therefore, if the headstay were loaded to 12,000 lbs, the tension on the bobstay, *AC*, would be 27,700 lbs, and the compression load on the bowsprit, *BC*, would be 29,400 lbs.

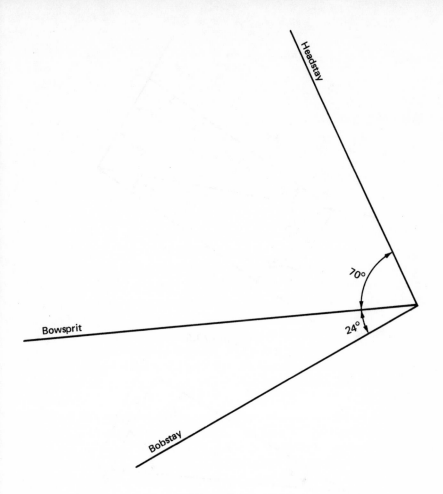

Headstay

70°

Bowsprit

24°

Bobstay

Figure 12-a

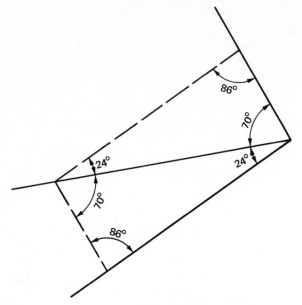

Figure 12-b

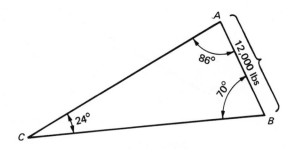

Figure 12-c

Other and more complex problems can be similarly solved. In some instances, drawing a rough diagram may assist in visualizing the problem.

Let us consider such a problem. A cargo boom is attached to a mast at deck level; the topping lift for the boom is attached to the mast 60 feet above the deck. The boom is 40 feet in length, and is topped up so that the falls hang 30 feet from the mast; *see* Figure 13-a. A 10-ton load is suspended from the boom. We wish to determine the tension on the topping lift and the compression load on the boom.

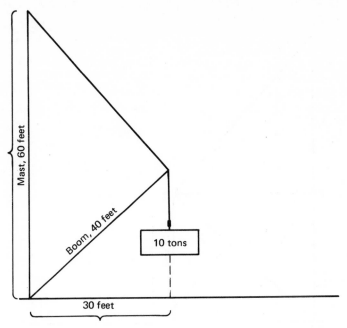

Figure 13-a

To help in visualizing the problem, it would be wise to make a sketch similar to Figure 13-b; it does not have to be carefully drawn.

The first step is to determine the angle the falls make with the boom; this is the angle *ABD* in Figure 13-b. The boom is 40 feet long, and the falls, which hang vertically, are centered 30 feet from the mast. By the law of sines, we therefore find the required angle, *ABD*

$$40 \text{ feet} : \sin 90° : : 30 \text{ feet} : \sin 48° 36'$$

The falls, therefore, hang at an angle of 48° 36′ relative to the boom. We also know now that the boom makes an angle, *CAB*, of 48° 36′ with the mast, because the latter and the falls are parallel; lastly, we know that the boom makes an angle, *BAD*, of 41° 24′ with the deck (90° − 48° 36′).

On the sketch, we draw a horizontal line, *BX*, from the top of the boom to the mast; this line will be the same length, 30 feet, as the distance from the mast to the point plumbed by the falls, *AD*. We now determine the height of the boom relative to the mast, *AX*, again by the law of sines, using the right triangle, *AXB*. Since the boom is 40 feet long, we write

$$\sin 90° : 40 \text{ feet} : : \sin 41° 24' : 26.4 \text{ feet}$$

167

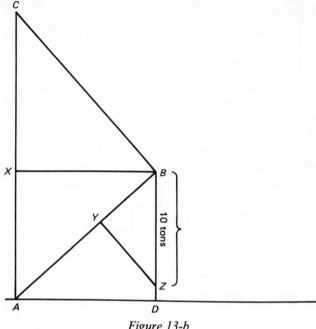

Figure 13-b

The horizontal line, *BX*, from the top of the boom therefore meets the mast 26.4 feet above the deck, and as the head of the mast is 60 feet above the deck, the head, *C*, is 33.6 feet above *X* (60′ − 26.′4).

Next we find the angle made by the topping lift with the mast, in the triangle *XCB*. As horizontal *XB* is 30 feet in length, and the head is 33.6 feet above where this line reaches the mast, the tangent of the angle *BCX* formed by the lift and the mast is $\frac{30 \text{ feet}}{33.6 \text{ feet}}$, or 0.893, which makes the angle 41° 46′.

By drawing a line, *YZ*, from the boom to the falls parallel to the topping lift *CB*, we have the triangle *BZY*, which enables us to determine the compression load on the boom, and the tension on the topping lift. If the length of the line *BZ* represents the 10-ton load, by the law of sines, the length *BY* represents the compression load on the boom, and the length *YZ* the tension on the lift. Since we have found the angle made by the mast and boom, *CAB*, to be 48° 36′, and as the falls and mast are parallel, the angle *YBZ* also is 48° 36′. Furthermore, the angle *YZB* must equal the angle

ACB formed by the mast and lift, which is 41°46'. In the triangle *BYZ*, *B* is 48°36' and *Z* is 41°46', the angle *Y*, therefore, must equal 89°38' [180° − (48°36' + 41°46')]. Using the law of sines we now write

$$\sin 89°38' \ (|\ Y) : 10 \text{ tons} :: \sin 41°46' \ (\underline{|Z}) : 6.66 \text{ tons } (BY)$$
$$:: \sin 48°36' \ (\underline{|B}) : 7.5 \text{ tons } (YZ)$$

Tension on the topping lift, *YZ*, therefore, is 7.5 tons, and the compression load on the boom, *BY*, is 6.66 tons.

By the same process, we could calculate the compression load on the mast, and the strain on a shroud or stay supporting the masthead, and opposite the topping lift. The solution would be as in the first example, in which, having been given the tension of a headstay, we calculated the compression load on the bowsprit and the tension on the bobstay.

In this latter example the mast is 60 feet in length, and the topping lift forms an angle of 41°46' with the mast. If a shroud or stay leads from the deck 30 feet from the mast to the masthead, and is directly opposite the lift, the compression load on the mast is 15.58 tons, and the tensile load on the shroud is 11.17 tons.

Span Loads

If the two parts of a span form equal angles with the vertical, each leg will carry an equal load. In many cases, however, this will not be so, and the loads on the legs will differ.

The load on each leg of a span can be readily calculated by means of the slide rule. The angle each part of the span forms with the vertical can usually be determined by eye with sufficient accuracy for practical purposes; in critical cases it should be determined by solution of right triangles.

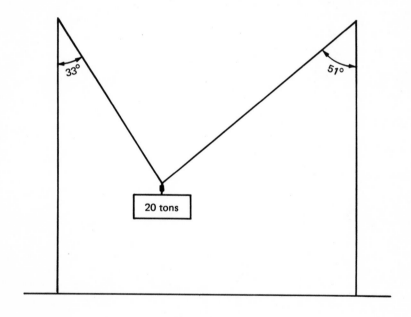

Figure 14-a

Let us suppose that a weight of 20 tons is suspended from a span, one part of which forms an angle of 33° with the vertical, while the other part forms an angle of 51° (*see* Figure 14-a), and we wish to determine the tension on each part of the span.

To assist in visualizing the problem you can sketch a triangle; *see* Figure 14-b. Side *c* is vertical, and its length represents the load of 20 tons. Side *a* represents the more nearly horizontal leg of the span; angle *B* is 51°. Side *b* represents the other leg of the span, and angle *A* is 33°. Angle *C*, therefore, must equal 96° [180° − (51° + 33°)]. Solution is by the law of sines, using 84° (180° − 96°) for angle *C*

$\sin 84°$ $\lfloor C$: 20 tons, *c* : : $\sin 51°$ $\lfloor B$: 15.63 tons, *b* : : $\sin 33°$ $\lfloor A$: 10.95 tons, *a*

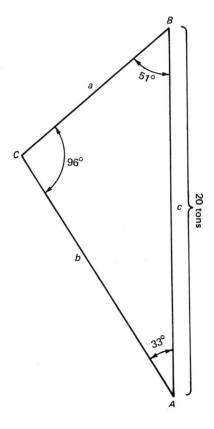

Figure 14-b

Bear in mind that the more nearly horizontal the legs of a span are, the greater will be the tension on each leg.

Thus, in the span we considered, if the angle each leg formed with the vertical were increased by 10°, so that they were 61° and 43°, the solution to the ratio would be that the tensile loads on the legs would increase to 18.03 tons and 14.06 tons, respectively.

Wind-Generated Pressure
on a Ship

Much study has been devoted to determining the force that winds exert on a vessel. Some findings have been contradictory, probably due to the great fluctuations in wind speed over a very brief period of time. However, it is believed that, under most conditions, the following formula will give acceptable results

$$P = 0.004 \times v^2$$

where P is the pressure in pounds per square foot of frontal area, and v is the wind velocity in knots.

For a vessel at anchor, P will be increased due to surge and yaw. With fresh winds, this factor may be considered to have a value of about 33%; under highly adverse conditions it may be much greater, if the vessel is yawing considerably. Excessive yawing may, of course, be reduced if two anchors, with considerable spread between them, are laid out.

Example: A vessel has a total frontal area of 2,500 square feet. What would be the approximate wind pressure on her if she were lying to a single anchor in a protected anchorage with a 30-knot wind blowing?

We would write the formula

$$P = 0.004 \times 2,500 \times 900 = 9,000$$

If she were lying true to the wind, the pressure generated by the wind would, therefore, be in the neighborhood of 9,000 lbs. If she were yawing somewhat, the pressure might approach 12,000 lbs.

Draft of a Steamer When Heeled

Ships that have more or less rectangular midships sections increase their draft when heeled. That increase may be approximated by the formula

$$\text{Increase in draft} = \text{sine angle of heel} \times \frac{\text{ship's beam}}{2}$$

Example: Our steamer has a beam of 64 feet 6 inches, and is drawing 24 feet 9 inches. We wish to determine her approximate draft when she is inclined 9°. The formula becomes

$$\text{Increase in draft} = \sin 9° \times \frac{64.5 \text{ feet}}{2} = 5.05$$

The increase in draft, therefore, is 5.05 feet, or 5 feet 0.6 inches. When the ship is heeled 9°, her approximate draft to the nearest inch will, therefore, be 29 feet 10 inches (24′9″ + 5′1″).

Sailing to Weather

It is axiomatic that success in the majority of sailing races hinges on the boat's performance to weather. With the mark dead to weather, if the boat can harden her wind slightly the distance to the mark is somewhat reduced. Conversely, if she must bear off, as in a steep head sea, in order to maintain speed, the distance to the mark is considerably increased.

The slide rule can be used to advantage to determine the increase or decrease in the distance to be sailed as the heading relative to the wind is changed. If the boat has a good speed log, the optimum heading on the wind can readily be determined. All that is required is to weigh changes in speed, considered as percentages, against changes in distance, also considered as percentages.

Leeway enters into the problem, but it is imponderable; it varies with hull form, wind speed, and sea state. Allowance for leeway must therefore be made by the skipper, based on his own experience. The only safe generality here is that for any given wind and sea condition, a sailboat tends to make less leeway when moving rapidly than when moving slowly.

The distance a boat must sail to reach a mark dead to weather is best expressed as a percentage of the actual distance to the mark. This percentage may be found by the formula

$$D = \frac{200}{\text{sine angle between boards}} \times \text{sine attack angle}$$

where D is the percentage of the distance to the mark, the angle between boards is the angle through which the boat tacks when on the wind, and the attack angle is the angle off the wind when sailing; that is to say, one half the angle between boards.

Example: We wish to determine the distance to be sailed to a mark 6.5 miles dead to weather if the boat tacks (1) through 84°, (2) through 90°, and (3) through 96°.

(1) In this case, the formula is written

$$D = \frac{200}{\sin 84°} \times \sin 42° = 134.6\%$$

and
$$6.5 \times 134.6 = 8.75$$

When tacking through 84°, therefore, we must sail 8.75 miles.

(2) Here, the formula is written

$$D = \frac{200}{\sin 90°} \times \sin 45° = 141.4\%, \text{ and } 6.5 \times 141.4 = 9.19$$

When tacking through 90°, therefore, we must sail 9.19 miles.

(3) In this instance, the formula is written

$$D = \frac{200}{\sin 96°} \times \sin 48° = 149.5\%$$

Note: The sine of 96° is, of course, the same as the cosine of 6°

$$6.5 \times 149.5\% = 9.72$$

When tacking through 96°, therefore, we must sail 9.72 miles.

It is obvious from the above solutions that a considerable increase in speed is necessary to justify bearing off from the normal attack angle. We can see that if we ordinarily tack through 90°, but then change, and tack through 96°, we must increase our speed by about 6% to justify the additional distance we must sail (9.19 : 100 : : 9.72 : 105.8).

Tacking Down Wind

When Lee Mark is Dead to Leeward

In light going, a sailboat running can ordinarily increase her speed if she hardens her wind. The problem then is to determine whether the increase in speed will more than offset the additional distance it will be necessary to sail to the mark after hardening up.

In considering this problem, vagaries of the weather must be ruled out, and, it must be assumed that the wind will remain steady both in direction and speed. When there is a shift in either wind force or direction, a new problem is created, and a new solution will be required. We will start by considering the problem when the next mark is dead to leeward.

The first step is to determine the increased speed for a given angle of divergence from the base course: usually this angle is 10°. This process is repeated as often as seems desirable, again ordinarily using increments of 10°, and noting the speed on each divergence angle.

In the interests of simplicity, we will assume that we will make only two legs in running to the mark. In practice, this might not be a desirable procedure, as it might take us too far from the rhumb line. For any given angle of divergence from the rhumb line, the distance sailed will remain the same, regardless of the number of legs.

The total distance sailed for a given angle of divergence from the base line can be determined from the following formula, which is based on the law of sines

$$\text{Total distance sailed} = \frac{2 \times \text{base distance} \times \text{sine divergence angle}}{\text{sine (divergence angle} \times 2)}$$

Knowing the speed for each divergence angle, and also the total distance to be sailed if that divergence is used, the divergence angle which will permit arrival at the lee mark in the least time can be readily determined.

Example: The lee mark is distant exactly 10 miles, and when we sail directly for it, our speedometer shows 5.0 knots. When we harden up 10°, our speed increases to 5.25 knots; hardened 20°, it is 5.65 knots, and at 30° it is 6.0 knots. What is the optimum divergence angle?

First we list the divergence angles, as shown below, and note the speed for each divergence angle. Next, we use the formula above to calculate the total distance sailed for each divergence angle, and note the results. Lastly, we determine how long it will take us to reach the mark for each divergence angle.

Divergence angle in degrees	Speed in knots or mph	Distance to sail in miles	Time required in hours
0	5.0	10.0	2.0
10	5.25	10.15	1.935
20	5.65	10.64	1.88
30	6.00	11.54	1.923

We will, we see, get to the mark in the least time if we harden our wind 20°.

When Lee Mark is Not Dead to Leeward

Determining the best course to select for tacking down wind, when the lee mark is not dead to leeward, presents a slightly different problem, as the two legs will not be of equal length. As a general rule, it would be wisest to sail directly for the mark unless the divergence between the course and the true wind is fairly small, say in the neighborhood of 10°.

Let us assume that such a divergence exists and that the wind will remain steady. To determine the gain to be derived from hardening up, we proceed as in the previous example to obtain our increase in speed, but in smaller increments, say 5° each.

We next calculate the distance to be sailed to the mark for each relative heading, bearing in mind that the headings relative to the wind must, in this case, be converted to headings relative to the base line to the lee mark, and that each heading relative to the wind must be solved for two headings relative to the base line. Thus, if the mark bears 000°, the wind is from 185° (or blowing in the direction 005°), and we propose to harden the wind 20°, the heading for the long leg would be 345° (005° − 20°), and that for the short leg would be 025° (005° + 20°). We have then, a triangle two of whose angles are 15° (360° − 345°) and 025°, and whose third angle must, consequently, be 140° [180° − (15° + 25°)].

The distances on the two headings can be determined by the law of sines

$$\sin \lfloor A : a : : \sin \lfloor B : b : : \sin \lfloor C : c$$

Set the sine of the angle between the two headings to the direct distance to the mark, and under the sine of the larger angle read the distance on the long leg, and under the sine of the smaller angle, read the distance on the short leg.

Enter these two distances, together with their sum, opposite the appropriate wind divergence angle on a form, as shown in the example below. The length of each leg, rather than only the sum of the two, should be entered, as it may be necessary to determine the time to gybe on the basis of the length of the first leg, or the time spent on the leg. Also enter the speed obtained on that divergence angle and the compass headings for the two legs.

Next, calculate the lengths of the legs when the wind is hardened an additional 5°, and enter them, together with their sum, the speed obtained on this divergence angle, and the compass headings for the two legs on the form. This process is repeated in 5° increments. The number of increments required will depend on the sailing characteristics of the boat, and can be determined only by experience.

The final step is to determine the time required to sail the two legs for each divergence angle at the speed obtained on that angle. This is done by means of the ratio

Speed : 1 hour, or 60 minutes : : Sum of distance on the two legs
: total time required   (1)

and these total times are entered in the form.

An inspection will then determine the wind divergence angle which will enable the boat to reach the lee mark in minimum time.

Example: The distance to the lee mark is 10.0 miles, and the direction is 090°. The true wind is from 260°, its divergence from the direction of the mark is therefore 10°. When sailing directly for the mark, our speed is 4.6 knots.

> After hardening up 5°, heading 095°, our speed is 4.9 knots
> After hardening up 10°, heading 100°, our speed is 5.25 knots
> After hardening up 15°, heading 105°, our speed is 5.45 knots

We require the optimum heading, to reach the mark in the least time.

As in the previous example, the first step is to determine the total distance we will have to sail each time we harden the wind, as well as the distance on each leg. In each instance, one long and one short leg will be involved;

however, if the distance is considerable, it will be wise to sail two or more long and two or more short legs, in order not to depart too far from the base line. In any case, the total distance to be sailed, as well as distance or distances to be sailed on the long and short legs may be obtained from a single solution for one long leg and one short leg.

We next determine what the compass headings will be for each divergence angle from the wind. In this example they will be 095° (080° + 15°) and 065° (080° − 15°), 100° and 060°, and 105° and 55°.

We enter these data in a form, as follows:

Headings	Divergence from wind in degrees	Speed in knots	Distance on long leg in miles	Distance on short leg in miles	Total distance in miles	Total time in minutes
090°	10	4.6			10	
095° and 065°	15	4.9				
100° and 060°	20	5.25				
105° and 055°	25	5.45				

We next calculate the lengths of the long and short legs for each divergence angle from the wind. Thus, when the wind divergence angle is 15°, our headings will be 095° and 065°; as the mark bears 090°, we will first be 5° and then 25° away from its present bearing. We thus have two angles whose sines will supply the lengths of the two legs, when used in conjunction with the direct distance to the mark, and the angle between the first leg, 095° and the second leg, 065°.

Using the law of sines and the ratio

$$\sin 30° : 10.00 \text{ miles} :: \sin 25° : \text{long leg, and } \sin 5° : \text{short leg} \qquad (2)$$

we find the long leg will be 8.45 miles, and the short leg will be 1.74 miles, making the total distance to be sailed 10.19 miles when we harden the wind 15°.

We repeat the process for the next wind divergence angle, 20°. In this instance the headings sailed will be 100° and 060°, so we will first sail 10° and then 30° away from the bearing of the mark. The difference between the two headings, 100° and 060°, is 40°. Using this, and the direct distance to the mark 10.00, by means of the law of sines, we find that the long leg will be 7.78 miles; and the short leg 2.70 miles, giving a total distance to sail of 10.48 miles.

The process is repeated a third time for a wind divergence angle of 25°. Here the headings sailed are 105° and 055°, and by the law of sines, we find the long leg to be 7.49 miles, and the short to be 3.38 miles, for a total distance sailed of 10.87 miles.

These data can now be entered in the appropriate columns in the form, and all that remains is to find the time required to reach the mark for the various wind divergence angles, using the ratio (1) above

Speed : 60 minutes : : distance : required time

Thus, for the wind divergence angle 15°, we have

4.9 knots : 60 minutes : : 10.19 miles : 124.75 minutes

For the wind divergence angle 20°, we have

5.25 knots : 60 minutes : : 10.48 miles : 119.7 minutes

and, coincidentally, the wind divergence angle of 25° also yields a time of 119.7 minutes.

These data are now entered in the form, as shown below, and we note that a wind divergence angle of 20° is the most desirable, as it combines the best obtainable elapsed time with the most direct route to the mark.

Headings	Divergence from wind in degrees	Speed in knots	Distance on long leg in miles	Distance on short leg in miles	Total distance in miles	Total time in minutes
090°	10	4.6	—	—	10.00	130.4
095° and 065°	15	4.9	8.45	1.74	10.19	124.75
100° and 060°	20	5.25	7.78	2.70	10.48	119.7
105° and 055°	25	5.45	7.49	3.38	10.87	119.7

The fact that the last two times are the same shows that we need not try additional headings, because the increased distances will offset any expected gains in speed.

Further, if no change in wind speed or direction could be foreseen, with two divergence angles which would permit us to reach the mark at the same time, we would, as a matter of sound racing tactics, select the one which kept us nearest to the base line to the mark.

This solution seems rather lengthy; however, with some practice, solutions to this type of problem may be obtained very rapidly.

A somewhat similar problem arises occasionally on a reach in light going, when the wind is a little too far forward to permit carrying a spinnaker. Under such conditions, it may pay to harden your wind somewhat and close reach above the direct course to the mark carrying a #1 Genoa, then bear off for the mark under a spinnaker when it will draw. If such a maneuver is adopted, the additional distance to be covered is determined as in the above problem.

Draft Variation of a Sailboat When Heeled

A deep-draft sailboat, when heeled, draws less than when she is upright. The exact reduction in draft depends on the shape of the cross section of the keel at its deepest point. However, the reduction can be closely approximated by the formula

Inclined draft = cosine angle of inclination × draft when upright

Example: Let us assume that, when upright, our sloop draws 6 feet, and we wish to determine her approximate draft when she is heeled 30°. We write the formula

Inclined draft = cos 30° × 6 feet = 5.2

When our sloop is heeled 30°, her approximate draft is, therefore, 5.2 feet, or 5 feet 2.4 inches.

If the boat has a keel of rectangular cross section and of known thickness, further refinement in determining draft when heeled may be obtained. The depth to be added to the inclined draft, as previously determined, may be found by the ratio

$$\sin 90° : \frac{\text{keel thickness}}{2} :: \sin \text{angle of inclination} : \text{additional depth}$$

Thus, if our sloop had such a keel 6 inches thick, for the above example we would write

sin 90° : 3 inches : : sin 30° : 1.5 inches

The increase in draft due to the keel thickness, therefore, is 1.5 inches, and the total draft at an angle of inclination of 30° would be 5 feet 3.9 inches.

Small angles of inclination achieve very little reduction in draft. Our boat, which normally draws 6 feet, would draw only slightly less than 5 feet 11 inches if heeled 10°, and if heeled 20°, her draft would be about 5 feet 7¾ inches. If we have the misfortune of putting her aground, and if the point of greatest draft is pretty well aft, it would be best first to try getting her off by putting the crew all the way forward in the eyes.

Decimals of an Hour into Minutes and Seconds

There is an increasing tendency to express minutes and seconds of time as decimals of an hour. In yacht racing, for instance, special decimal timers are used to facilitate the calculation of time allowances: in many of the major long-distance races, both elapsed times and corrected times are now stated in decimals, usually to four places.

At times it is desirable to convert such decimal time to minutes and seconds; this can be done with considerable accuracy by means of the slide rule. In making this conversion, it should be borne in mind that the first two decimal places represent minutes and decimals of a minute, and the following decimals represent seconds and decimals of a second.

The easiest way to convert decimals of an hour with the slide rule is to multiply the first two digits in the decimal by 60 to obtain minutes and decimals of a minute. The number of whole minutes is noted, and the decimals of a minute are multiplied by 60 to convert them to seconds. Thus, if 0.7926 hours are to be converted, 0.79 is multiplied by 60, and 47.4 minutes are obtained; 0.4 is then multiplied by 60, and becomes 24 seconds. We note 47 minutes 24 seconds. Then we convert 0.0026 to seconds by multiplying it by 3600, the number of seconds in an hour, and we obtain 9.36 seconds. We now have 47 minutes 24 seconds (+) 9 seconds, or 47 minutes 33 seconds.

Example: We wish to convert 0.8197 hours to minutes and seconds.

$$0.81 \times 60 = 48.6 \text{ minutes} = 48 \text{ minutes } 36 \quad \text{seconds}$$
$$0.0097 \times 3600 \qquad\qquad = \underline{\qquad\qquad 34.9 \text{ seconds}}$$
$$49 \text{ minutes } 10.9 \text{ seconds}$$

We would, therefore, say that 0.8197 hours equalled 49 minutes 11 seconds.

In converting minutes and seconds to decimals of an hour with the slide rule, the easiest method is to use ratios; however, the error in the result is apt to be greater than when converting decimals of hours into minutes and seconds.

To convert minutes to decimals of an hour, 60 on the **C** scale is set against the right index of **D**, and under the number of minutes on **C**, the equivalent decimal is found on **D**, and is noted. Seconds are converted to decimals by setting 3,600 on **C** against the index of **D**, and under the number of seconds on **C** the decimal is found on **D**. This is added to the decimal value of the minutes previously found.

Example: We wish to convert 53 minutes 37 seconds to decimals of an hour. Then

$$60 : 1 :: 53 : 0.8830$$
and
$$3600 : 1 :: 37 : 0.0103$$
$$\overline{0.8933}$$

Therefore, 53 minutes and 37 seconds = 0.8933 hours.

This value is in error by 0.0003 hours, or about one second. Greater accuracy may be obtained by use of the table given below. To convert 53 minutes 37 seconds to decimals of an hour by this method, we would first extract from the table the decimal equivalent of 50 minutes and note it, as shown below. Next, we would take out the value of 3 minutes, then of 30 seconds, and finally of 7 seconds. The sum of the decimals gives us the answer we require.

	Minutes	Seconds	Hours
	50		= 0.8333
	3		= 0.0500
		30	= 0.0083
		7	= 0.0019
Therefore,	53	37	= 0.8935

which is correct to 0.0001, or a small fraction of a second.

Minutes and Seconds as Decimals of an Hour

Minutes		Hours	Seconds		Hours
1	=	0.0167	1	=	0.0003
2	=	0.0333	2	=	0.0006
3	=	0.0500	3	=	0.0008
4	=	0.0667	4	=	0.0011
5	=	0.0833	5	=	0.0014
6	=	0.1000	6	=	0.0017
7	=	0.1167	7	=	0.0019
8	=	0.1333	8	=	0.0022
9	=	0.1500	9	=	0.0025
10	=	0.1667	10	=	0.0028
20	=	0.3333	20	=	0.0056
30	=	0.5000	30	=	0.0083
40	=	0.6667	40	=	0.0111
50	=	0.8333	50	=	0.0139

Conversion Tables

The following conversion tables for length, mass, speed, and volume have been adapted from the Corrected Reprint, 1962, of U.S. Naval Oceanographic Office, H.O. Publication No. 9 (Bowditch).

Length

		Equivalent Values to Five Decimal Places		Slide-Rule Settings
1 inch	=	25.4	millimeters*	1:25.4
1 inch	=	2.54	centimeters*	1:2.54
1 foot	=	0.3048	meters*	2:0.61
1 yard	=	0.9144	meters*	7:6.4
1 fathom	=	6	feet*	1:6
1 fathom	=	1.8288	meters*	1:1.83
1 cable (U.S.)	=	720	feet*	1:720
1 cable (British)	=	0.1	nautical miles*	1:0.1
1 cable (British)	=	607.6	feet	7:4,250
1 statute mile	=	5,280	feet*	7:37,000
1 statute mile	=	1,609.344	meters*	1:1,610
1 statute mile	=	0.86898	nautical miles	1:0.87

* Exact relationship.

Length—*Continued*

		Equivalent Values to Five Decimal Places		*Slide-Rule Settings*
1 nautical mile	=	6,076.11549	feet	7:42,500
1 nautical mile	=	2,025.37183	yards	2:4,050
1 nautical mile	=	1,852.0	meters*	1:1,850
1 nautical mile	=	1.15078	statute miles	1:1.15
1 meter	=	39.37008	inches	1:39.4
1 meter	=	3.28084	feet	1:3.28
1 meter	=	1.09361	yards	3:3.28
1 meter	=	0.54681	fathoms	1:0.55
1 kilometer	=	3,280.83990	feet	1:3,280
1 kilometer	=	1,093.61330	yards	3:3,280
1 kilometer	=	0.62137	statute miles	7:4.35
1 kilometer	=	0.53996	nautical miles	1:0.54

Mass

1 ounce	=	437.5	grains*	4:1,750
1 ounce	=	28.34952	grams	3:85
1 ounce	=	0.0625	pounds*	2:0.125
1 pound	=	7,000	grains*	1:7,000
1 pound	=	0.45359	kilograms	3:1.36
1 short ton	=	2,000	pounds*	1:2,000
1 short ton	=	907.18474	kilograms*	3:2,720
1 short ton	=	0.90718	metric tons	3:2.72
1 short ton	=	0.89286	long tons	3:2.68
1 displacement ton	=	2,240	pounds*	1:2,240
1 long ton	=	2,240	pounds*	1:2,240
1 long ton	=	1.12	short tons*	1:1.12
1 long ton	=	1,016.04691	kilograms	6:6,100
1 long ton	=	1.01605	metric tons	6:6.1
1 kilogram	=	2.20462	pounds	1:2.20
1 kilogram	=	0.00110	short tons	1:0.0011
1 kilogram	=	0.00098	long tons	1:0.00098

* Exact relationship.

Mass—*Continued*

		Equivalent Values to Five Decimal Places	Slide-Rule Settings
1 metric ton	=	1,000 kilograms*	1:1,000
1 metric ton	=	2,204.62262 pounds	1:2,200
1 metric ton	=	1.10231 short tons	1:1.1
1 metric ton	=	0.98421 long tons	6:5.9

Speed

1 yard per minute	=	0.03409 statute miles per hour	1:0.034
1 yard per minute	=	0.02962 knots	5:0.149
1 yard per minute	=	0.01524 meters per second*	4:0.061
1 statute mile per hour	=	88 feet per minute*	1:88
1 statute mile per hour	=	29.33333 yards per minute	3:88
1 statute mile per hour	=	1.60934 kilometers per hour	1:1.61
1 statute mile per hour	=	1.46667 feet per second	3:4.4
1 statute mile per hour	=	0.86898 knots	1:0.87
1 statute mile per hour	=	0.44704 meters per second*	3:1.34
1 knot	=	1.68781 feet per second	8:1.35
1 knot	=	101.26859 feet per minute	8:810
1 knot	=	33.75620 yards per minute	4:135
1 knot	=	1.852 kilometers per hour*	2:3.7
1 knot	=	1.15078 statute miles per hour	1:1.5
1 knot	=	0.51444 meters per second	7:3.6
1 kilometer per hour	=	0.62137 statute miles per hour	7:4.35
1 kilometer per hour	=	0.53996 knots	1:0.54
1 meter per second	=	196.85039 feet per minute	3:5.9
1 meter per second	=	65.61680 yards per minute	9:590
1 meter per second	=	3.6 kilometers per hour*	1:3.6
1 meter per second	=	3.28084 feet per second	1:3.28
1 meter per second	=	2.23694 statute miles per hour	8:17.9
1 meter per second	=	1.94384 knots	5:9.7

* Exact relationship.

Volume

1 cubic foot	=	1,728 cubic inches*	7:12,100
1 cubic foot	=	7.48052 U.S. gallons	2:15
1 cubic foot	=	6.22884 British imperial gallons	2:12.45
1 cubic foot	=	0.02832 cubic meters	3:0.085
1 cubic foot	=	28.31606 liters	3:85
1 cubic yard	=	46,656 cubic inches*	3:140,000
1 cubic yard	=	201.97401 U.S. gallons	1:202
1 cubic yard	=	168.17859 British imperial gallons	6:1,010
1 cubic yard	=	0.76455 cubic meters	2:1.53
1 cubic yard	=	764.53368 liters	2:1,530
1 cubic meter (stere)	=	264.17203 U.S. gallons	7:1850
1 cubic meter (stere)	=	219.96924 British imperial gallons	1:220
1 cubic meter (stere)	=	35.31467 cubic feet	3:106
1 cubic meter (stere)	=	1.30795 cubic yards	1:1.31
1 U.S. gallon	=	3,785.39848 cubic centimeters	7:26,500
1 U.S. gallon	=	231 cubic inches*	1:231
1 U.S. gallon	=	0.13368 cubic feet	4:0.535
1 U.S. gallon	=	3.78531 liters	5:18.9
1 U.S. gallon	=	0.83267 British imperial gallons	6:5
1 British imperial gallon	=	1.20095 U.S. gallons	5:6
1 liter	=	1,000.028 cubic centimeters	1:1,000
1 liter	=	1.05672 U.S. quarts	7:7.4
1 liter	=	0.26418 U.S. gallons	5:1.32
1 register ton	=	100 cubic feet*	1:100
1 register ton	=	2.83168 cubic meters*	3:8.5
1 measurement ton	=	40 cubic feet*	1:40
1 measurement ton	=	1 freight ton*	1:1
1 freight ton	=	40 cubic feet*	1:40
1 freight ton	=	1 measurement ton*	1:1

* Exact relationship.

Speed of Sound

Sound in dry air at 60° F. and standard sea-level pressure	=	1,116.99	feet per second	6:6,700
	=	761.59	statute miles per hour	5:3,800
	=	661.80	knots	6.5:4,300
	=	340.46	meters per second	5:1,700
Sound in 3.485% salt water at 60° F.	=	4,945.37	feet per second	9:44,500
	=	1,648.46	yards per second	2:3,300
	=	3,371.85	statute miles per hour	8:27,000
	=	2,930.05	knots	3:8,800
	=	1,507.35	meters per second	1:1,510

Volume Mass

1 cubic foot of sea water	=	64	pounds	1:64
1 cubic foot of fresh water	=	62.428	pounds at temperature of maximum density (4°C = 39.°2 F.)	8:500
1 cubic foot of ice	=	56	pounds	1:56
1 displacement ton	=	35	cubic feet of sea water	1:35
	=	1	long ton	

Composed in ten point Times Roman with two points of leading by Tinker N.A. Corporation New York, New York.

Printed offset on sixty pound White Naval Hi Bulk and printed by Collins Lithographing and Printing Company, Incorporated, Baltimore, Maryland. Bound in 17 point Columbia Tanalin by Moore and Company, Incorporated, Baltimore, Maryland.